COSTUMES OF INDIAN TRIBES

COSTUMES OF INDIAN TRIBES

Edited by

Dr. Prakash Chandra Mehta

M.Sc. (Mathematics), M.A. (Economics), Ph.D.

DISCOVERY PUBLISHING HOUSE PVT. LTD.

NEW DELHI-110 002

Published by:
Tilak Wasan

DISCOVERY PUBLISHING HOUSE PVT. LTD.
4831/24, Prahlad Street, Ansari Road
Darya Ganj, New Delhi-110002 (India)
Phone : +91-11-23279245, 43764432
Fax : +91-11-23253475
E-mail : parul.wasan@gmail.com
discoverypublishinghouse@gmail.com
info@discoverypublishinggroup.com
web : www.discoverypublishinggroup.com

First Edition: 2011
ISBN: 978-81-8356-758-9

Costumes of Indian Tribes

Printed at:
Shree Balaji Art Press
Delhi

Preface

The tribals are an intrinsic part of our national life with their rich cultural heritage. They contribute a share of about eight per cent population and spread over about 45 part (19 per cent) of country's land with more than 500 tribal groups. They speak over 150 languages and 225 subsidiary languages. Every tribal group having special costumes. The costumes of every tribal group is different and it pay them special identity. The patterns of costumes of every tribal group differs from tribe-to-tribe and region-to-region.

Clothing is an expression of the person, reflecting personality, way of living and way of thinking, pride in self or family. The clothing should be no more than a tool, an aid in expressing what and who the person is. It is a reflection of one's tate and values. The tribal use minimum number of clothes and also were short length clothes. Their dressing pattern/costumes are purely different to the general people.

Keeping in view the importance of costumes, there is a gap in the literature. This work was a challenging task for me to collect photographs and details about the costumes of every tribal group. This was a voluminous work. So I have decided to work on prominent tribal groups residing in different parts of the country.

In this volume the learned scholars have discussed the consumes of different tribal groups spread over different part of the country.

I hope this volume will be milestone in the cultural heritage of Indian Tribes and provide adequate knowledge to Sociologists, Anthropologists and learned scholars about the costumes of Indian Tribes. I am grateful to all friends who have encouraged me in this onerous task. I indebted to Shri Tilak Vasan of M/s Discovery Publishing House, New Delhi for efficient publication. I am also thankful to my family members—wife Smt. Yashoda, daughters Smt. Sangeeta Nalwaya and Smt. Dr. Sonu Mehta, son Dr. Anurag and Kids Saloni, Mitali and Master Somaya—for their inspiration and association.

Dr. Prakash Chandra Mehta
45, Ravindranagar
Udaipur (Raj)-313003
Tel. (0294) 2490417 (Res.)
Mob.: 98872-67147

Contents

Contributors

1. Dr. Atul Chandra Bhowmick
Uttarayan, Palta
P.O. Bengal Enamal-743122
North 24 Parganas, West Bengal
2. Dr. (Mrs.) Bindu Ramachandran
Lecturer,
Dept. of Anthropology, Kan nur University
P.O. Palayad, Thalasserry
Kerala-700016
3. Dr. Nabakumar Duary
Anthropological Survey of India
27, Jawaharlal Nehru Road,
Kolkata (W.B.)
4. Dr. Basanta Kumar Mohanta
Indira Gandhi Rashtriya Manav Sangrahalaya,
Shamla Hills, Post Bag No. 2,
Bhopal (M.P.)-462013
5. Dr. Prakash Chandra Mehta
45, Ravindranagar, Udaipur (Raj.)-313003
6. Dr. (Mrs.) Sonu Mehta
Guest Lecturer, Home Science College,
MPUT, Udaipur
19, Mahaveer Colony, Hiran Magri,
Sector-4, Udaipur (Raj.)

Prologue

Clothing is an expression of the person, reflecting personality, way of living, way of thinking and especially, pride in self or family. Thus clothing should be no more than a tool, an aid in expressing what and who the person is. It is a reflection of one's tate, personality, life and values.

The costumes were developed as a result of man's narcissism, that is his pleasure in his own body and desire to make himself attractive as possible physically. According to Dr. John Carl Flugel narcissism is natural expression in the showing of the naked body and in the demonstration of its powers. Dr. Flugel in his book *The Psychology of Clothes*, commented that nacrassism can be observed in many children.

Consciously or unconsciously, people are at just interested in clothes and ornaments for enhancing the impressiveness of the body, but time by tim7e they develop an interest in costumes for their own sake and use a number of fashionable clothes. According to Dr. Flugel, the shift in interest from exhibition to costumes is comparatively less in women than a men, there is always greater readiness in women to combine displaced exhibition with actual exposure.

Traditionally, people are more tolerant of narcissism in women than a men, and this difference is revealed in costumes. The western people are especially idealized the rounded female form and has been some what critical of male physique with its greater angularity, hairiness, etc.

Attractiveness

Clothing originated in mam's desire to play up his own physical charms and make himself more attractive to others, especially to the opposite sex. Among savages (primitives) body decoration starts at or near the genital organs and often issued in connection with a ceremony celebrating the attainment of some stage in sexual development, as the arrival of puberty or selection of a mate. Dr. Flugel has written regarding this issue that the ultimate purpose of clothes, and often ended their overt and conscious purpose, is to add to the sexual attractiveness to the opposite sex and the envy of rivals of the same sex.

The primitive peoples interest in body decoration seems to be the main motive for dress. Some tribes paint their bodies or tattooo on themselves an all over pattern to enhance their own physical attractiveness, this pattern is very much popular among the African tribal groups and every tribal group has peculiar identity regarding this matter, Tattooting and painting have also been used to show tribal connections and rank within the tribe.

Very early, apparently, men and women began to use to cover the genital organs by leafs, *khals* of wild animals and *chhals* of trees. They also use shells, bones and similar ornaments to hang upon themselves a strophies of the hunts. The tribal people of both the sexes wear rings on fingers, anckees, necks, wasteland hips. This practice can be seen in the remote parts of the tribal belts even today.

Comfort

Comfort regarding costumes rates higher than in the past, especially for recreation and for casual use. In general the person wants that costumes must be comfortable and do not create any hurdle i.e. restrict movement and the fabric used must also be good to the skin, warmth in winter and coolness in summer within limits.

Whatever, might be the origin of the costumes provide the visible intex of homogeneity and the unity of people.

Costume conveys more than clothing. It also includes coiffure and ornaments. Coiffure refers to headdress and hair style, while ornaments are used for decoration of the body parts, it includes jewellery, tattooing, body painting etc.

As with the passage of time the change in the costume is widely visible. This change among the general people is more than comparatively to the trible people. The change among the tribals reside nearby the urban area can be seen more comparatively the tribals of the remote areas. Even today the tribals of the remote areas use their traditional costumes.

Indian Traditional Costumes

Traditional costumes of country varies across the regions in its colours and designs, and it depends on various other factors, including climate. The traditional *sari* and *salwar-kameez* are popular styles of dress of women. Traditional railments of men are *dhoti* and *kurta*. The dress varies widely throughout the country, where both traditional and western-style clothing are common.

Women in the country may generally wear *sari,* the length of *sari* varies from place to place. In north India generally women wear five meter long *sari*, while in Maharashtra they wear 8-10 meter long *sari*. In some parts women wear 2.5 meter to 3 meter long *sari*. The length of *sari* is wrapped over a petticoat and a bodice or *choli.* The style of wearing *sari* differs from region to region. The *salwar-kameej* is most common in the north-western part of the country.

The women of Rajasthan and Gujarat wear colourful swirling skirts called *lengha,* paired with a short bodice or *choli.* On the place of long *sari* they wear *odhani* having 2.5 meter to 3 meter in length and 1.5 meter in width. The most common male attire consists of *dhoti* and *kurta,* worn in most of the western and central regions. In southern part of the country *lungi* is worn by the male. The dressing pattern depending on the social practices of the region, it may be restricted to indoor-wear. As with the women's clothing jeans and other types of western-wear are very common in the metropolitan cities and smaller cities also; while shirts and pants are ubiquitous in cities and towns. Many Indian men and women wear traditional costumes around the world.

The costumes of tribals differ from general mass costumes. They generally use short clothes. The females wear their traditional costumes. They also use short length dresses. Every tribal group have different pattern of costumes. This practice may be seen throughout the country. So the dressing pattern including costumes give special identity to each tribal group and special indentity to the region.

CHAPTER 1

Adiyan, Mullukurumba and Kattunaicken

Dr. (Mrs.) Bindu Ramchandran

ADIYAN

The Adiyan are notified as a scheduled tribe inhabiting the Manantavady Taluk and adjoining areas of Wayanad district in Kerala. They were subjected to worst form of bonded labour till 1976. The landlords addressed the tied labourers as *kundalpanikkar* and the payment was known as *kundaipanam*. Bonded labour was referred to as *kundalpani* or *ballipani*. *Bally* was the wage received in kind often as paddy and *kundal* was the annual reward given to the labourers by their landlords. In addition to the normal wage the labourers were also allowed to harvest a small patch of land by themselves for their own use. They were a landless agricultural labourer community devoid of any other skill for their subsistence. Their culture and economy were languished by the traits of bonded labour system.

Luiz (1962) has observed that their name has originated from an old rule that they should maintain a distance of *ar* (six), *adi* (feet) to avoid pollution. The very name Adiyar connotes their subservient position as tied labourers. They were also known as *ravular* which means the descendants or *ramaswami*. Local communities address them as *adiyar*. Adiya language has close affinity to Kannada belonging to the Dravidian family of languages. Now most of them are bilingual. They can also speak Malayalam and use the Malayalam script.

The traditional manner of recruiting the tribals as bonded labourer was by advancing loans at the *Valliyoor Kavu Bhagavathi* temple (situated in the Manantavady taluk of Wayanad) in the last week of March. The system was that a tribal pledged not only himself but the members of his family as well against loan and until the debt was discharged all of them were bound to work for the creditor for which they got only daily meals and a pittance in kind (Mathur, 1997-98).

Origin

There are many myths and legends about the origin of Adiyan. According to one, "they are the descendants of a *Sivadwaja Brahmin* who ventured on a *prothiloma* a union (violating) the rule of hypergammy) with a pure non-Brahmin girl". Another legend is that they are the progeny of a Brahmin who lost his status by eating rice offered to Siva and thereby committed an *anacharam* (violation of a restricted custom). They also claim that at one time they were *pujaris* (priest in the *Bhadrakali* temple). It is perhaps true that they came to Kerala with the Chettis and Brahmins of Mysore and continued to be their agricultural serfs (Luiz, 1962: 27-28).

Clan

Family among the Adiyan is matrilineal in descent and matrilocal in residence. Nuclear family is the basic social and economic unit. Husband is the head of the family and division of labour in a family is based according to age and sex.

The society of adiyan is endogamous and divided into clans and phrateries. In their vernacular these matrilineal clans are known as *Manti* and phrateries as *Chemmem.* Each Mant and Chemmen are associated with a place name or the direction one points. Each Chemmem is exogamous in nature.

The three Mant (clan) are (*a*) Thirunelli mant, (*b*) Badak mant, and (*c*) Pothur mant. Among the three mant, Thirunelli mant is having higher social status. There are nineteen Chemmems in thirunelli mant with its own gods and goddesses. Badak mant have six Chemmems and Pothur mant have four Chemmems respectively. The chemmems of thirunelli mant are kottla, cheruvali, ulankuttu, muthukuttu, kuppala, kalankot, muthira, momatta, idamalai, madacheri, kachala, kadamala, naalapadi, maragavu, saitya, thirumunda, karai and kallumalai.

Chemmems of Badak mant constitute *bayanattila, kunduru, puthuru, poothadi, anjila* and *panalila.* Whereas Pothur mant consisted of our Chemmems i.e. aevila, vellachal, orpathukudi and pavadalam.

The members of a Chemmem are considered as brothers and sisters and no marriage is allowed i.e. Chemmems are strictly exogamous. Among the thirtyone Chemmem, some are treated as siblings and marriage is prohibited between them.

Siblings Chemmem which do not intennary are as follows:

Kottala	....	Cheruvai
Ulankuttu	....	Muthukuttu
Kallala	....	Kalakotae
Muthira	....	Momattae
Idamalai	....	Madacheri
Kachala	....	Kadamalai
Nalappadi	....	Maragavu
Saintya	....	Thirumunda
Karae	....	Kallumali
Puthuru	....	Poothadi
Anjila	....	Panalila
Aevila	....	Vellachal
Onpathukudi	....	Pavadalam

LIFE-CYCLE

Birth

Like other ceremonies, the birth ceremony is not at all important among Adiyan. There is no difference in the ceremonies for male and female child. When a woman gets labour pain she is confined to a room and seek the help of *bethikarathi* (midwife) who helps the mother in child birth. The midwife cuts the umbilical cord with a knife. The knife is not washed for five days. The newly delivered woman is considered to be polluted for five days. No one enters that room and no male members have their food from that house for five days.

On the fifth day, the *bethikarathi* cleans the house with cowdung, washes all the clothes and mats used by the mother and the child in river water, take her bath and returns. Then she breaks a coconut in the name of god and distributes the pieces to all children and present there. This is the only religious ceremony performed in order to remove the pollution associated with child birth. The *bethikarathi* is given betel leaves, are canuts lime, paddy, salt, oil, chilli, coconuts, soap and rupees forty by the mother-in-law on the fifth day.

On the fifth day *bethikarathi* ties a black string around the waist, on the ankle and on the arm of the child. In olden days they used to feed the newly born child at home. It is the child's father who keeps the child on his lap and feeds him first followed by others. During this ceremony the child is named.

There are no special ceremonies connected with the first hair cutting and ear boring. Either the father or mother cuts the hair of the child after one year. If there is any vow it is done in the temple.

Marriage

The usual form of marriage among the adiyar is described as one of service. As a preliminary step of fixation, boy's father, elder sister's husband and mother's brother visit the girl's hamlet. If they agreed to proceed that proposal, then the boy and some of his close relatives visit to the girl's house.

The boy must carry articles such as paddy, chilly, salt, betel leaves, onion and firewood. It is a kind of payment known as *kolubally* (*kolu* means firewood and *bally* means paddy).

After reaching the girl's house the boy presents the *kolubally* to the girl's mother and he distributes betel leaves to the invitees. He brings a *thali* (sacred thread) with coins (below ten in number) to tie around the girl's neck. Thali is handed over to the girl's father and he asks one of the women to tie it. Generally thali is tied by the boy's sister. It is customary to bring/*mookubettu* (nosestud), *kathala* (earstud), *kadagam (bangle)* and new dress to the bride. The thali is not destroyed or removed till puberty ceremony. After *thalikettu* (trying of thali) a feast is given to the invitees. Then the boy's party returns to their native hamlet.

Once this thali ceremony is performed, the boy has to observe certain rules and regulations. He must go to the house of the girl's once in a week usually on sundays with *kolubally.* When he reaches the girl's house, her parents entertain him and give him an axe to collect firewood from the nearby forest. If the bundle is also small the girl's relatives tease him.

The boy stays there and he is given *nookan* (rice with curry). It is served by the girl's mother. This custom continues till marriage. He visit all sundays with *kolubally* and returns on Monday. Even though he stays there every week he avoids physical contact with his would be bride or wife. Marriage is conducted only after the attainment of puberty. *Kolubally* cannot be equated with bride price. In many cases even after the payment of *kolubally* many girls refuse to marry the betrothed boy and ran away with another one.

Before marriage the consent of the *chemmekkaran* and *naattumoopan* is indispensable. *Naattumoopan* collects brass bangles from both the parties. It is known as *bethanum* Unless this is paid, *naattumoopan* will not give his consent for the marriage. The number of bangles depend on the quality of disputes. It is considered as a customary payment to *nattumoopan* and to his assistants for settling the disputes at the time of marriage. He may sometimes impose *thappu* (fine) on both the parties depending upon committed by them and they are freed from such offence through *thappedukkal* (imposition of fine). Fine paid by the groom goes to the girl's Chemmem and the fine paid by the bride goes to the groom's Chemmem.

Marriage ceremony always begins at night. It is concluded at the house of the *Chemmakkaran.* It is his responsibility to conduct the function in his *Chemmem.* When the bride leaves the home for marriage, elders bless her by sprinkling rice on her head. This is known as *ariyidal.* The groom's party carries a '*thudi*' (a kind of musical instrument) and *Cheeni* (a musical instrument) along with them. As this beating progresses, one of them starts performing a dance called *paygavanattam.* The dancer is called *paygavan.* He has a different dress. A red mundu with a belt is tied over the mundu. Besides this dance they sing many songs narrating the myth of their ancestors. After reaching the bride's residence, the bridegroom distributes betel leaves and *arecanut* to all the invitees. *Naattumoopan* and his assistants sacrifice a fowl and roast it. This is to avoid all problems at the time of marriage.

After taking bath, bride and groom are covered in a canopy of white dress on both sides of their way and walk over another white cloth spread on their way. This is known as *paavadapudikkal.* After that they are seated in the *pandal* (temporary shed). Then the *Chemmakkaran* of the groom calls the groom's sister for tying *thali* (sacred thread). After *thali* tying ceremony *naattumoopan* breaks a coconut and dips a betel leaf in the coconut water and sprinkles it on the bride and groom. After marriage a feast is given to all the invitees. Serving is carried out by males only.

When they reach the groom's residence. The party is received by the groom's relatives. A ceremonial bath is given there also. It is believed that only after this bath she is admitted in their *Chemmem.* On the second day of marriage, the couple enter a separate room with some of the old women of the house. The women advised them about the future life. This is known as *buddiparayal.*

Adiyans are monogamous by custom. One is permitted to have a second wife only after divorce. If one husband marries another married women, it is considered as a fault and he will have to pay fine. Fine is paid in the form of brass bangles which is around sixteen in number.

When the groom is unable to pay *kolubally,* he serves for the parents of the bride. The service is rendered till marriage is conducted. Elopement is an approved form of marriage among adiyan. If the closed couple are previously married, it is the duty of the *karimi* and *nattumoopan* to protect them upto a function called *kunnukayattal* (taking the new couple to the hamlet). It is a function for giving social recognition. One who breaks the rule for exogamy will have to give thirty brass bangles as fine. They are excommunication if they are not willing to give this fine.

Death

A death in a settlement is first informed to the *kuntumoopan* and to the *naattumoopan. Naattumoopan* arrange two *karimis* (assistants) to two directions for informing the relatives of the dead. A wooden stick called *kuntham vadi* is also carried by the *karimi.* Kins are not allowed to touch the dead body. That right is betowed to *karimis* of idamalai Chemmem. After the corpse is given bath, *naattumoopan* sent two *karimis* to collect bamboo stretcher called *padi* to take the corpse to the burial ground. Then *naattumoopan* asks for *thappubalai* (brass bangles given as fine). Three *thappubalai* are given in the name of three *man,* eight are given to the father's relatives of the deceased, and six are given to the *Chemmakkaran* of the deceased. These *thappubalai* are collected by *naattumoopan.*

The corpse is given bath in hot water in a sitting posture facing east. Turmeric paste and oil are applied on the body.

After bath, if the disease is a female, the corpse is covered by black *sari*, and if the deceased is a male his face is shaved and applied sandal paste. The corpse is then taken to the courtyard and laid down keeping head towards south. Rice, coins, six *thappubalai* and a bell metal lamp are kept close to the head. The body is covered with white cloth. *Naattumoopan* and *kanaladi* start reciting mantras. The *karini* then lay the corpse on *padi* made for the purpose and *thappubalai* are tied on the four corners of the stretcher. Then *kuntumoopan* throw few coins upwards. This is repeated by *Chemmakkaran* of the decased, brothers and father of the deceased, if alive and lastly *naattumoopan,* the ownership right of these coins goes to *karimis.*

Then the four *karimis* takes four sides of the reed stretcher containing corpse and it is taken to graveyard. They dig a grave and the corpse is lowered in to the grave and pushed into the cellar. Before covering the grave, a *thappubalai* is placed under the head of the corpse. A soil heap of six inch thickness is prepared on the grave and thorns are kept over it. This thickness is prepared on the grave and thorns are kept over it. This is in order to keep the dead man's soul confined to the grave as the soul is believed to be trying to return with the living ones.

Karimi stands on the head portion of the grave and then he sprinkle water which was kept in a piece of reed with grass on the body of *kuntumoopan, chemmakkaran,* and close relatives starts observing death pollution. The duration of pollution and the subsequent observances varies in accordance with financial status of the family.

The *karimis* exchange knife and axe by standing two opposite sides of the grave. The relatives take bath after the burial and everybody return to the dead person's house and *naattumoopan* and others settles the payments towards the burial. Twentyseven *thappubalai* are given for preparing *padi,* ten for digging grave, one for bringing sandal paste smeared over the forehead and eight for other related rites. *Nattumoopan* asked *kuntumoopan* to fix a date for the observance of pula within three days and the assembled persons disperse.

MULLUKURUMBA

The major concentration of the Mullukurumba are in the Wayanad district of Kerala state. They are also settled in Gudallur Taluk of Nilgiri district of Tamil Nadu. The census report of 1961 have not recorded Mullukurumba as a separate tribe. They are in all probability included either under Kurumans or Kurumbas. Aiyappan (1948: 92) calls them as one of the tribes of Wayanad, and Luiz (1962: 197), Rajalakshmi Misra (1971: 1) describes them as the inhabitants of Calicut, Cannanore districts and also adds they are a district tribe. There are a number of oral and written stories regarding the origin of this tribe. Thurston quotes from the Madras census report 1891... "... the Kurumans or Kurumans are the modern representatives of the ancient Kurumbas or Pallavas who were once so powerful thought of southern India, but very little trace of their greatness now remains.... The final overthrow of the Kurumba sovereignty was effected by the Chola king Adondai about the 17th or 18th century A.D., and the Kurumbas were scattered far and wide. Many fled to the hills and in the Nilgiris and the Wayanad, in Coorg and Mysore, representatives of this ancient race are now found as wild and uncivilized tribes" (1909).

Generally the social organisation of the Mullukurumba revolves around the nuclear family, and, father is the head of the family. They are a patrilineal and patrilocal society. They trace their descent through female line, but succession and inheritance is through the male line. Society is divided into four clans, known as *'kulam'* i.e., vadakkakulam, villippakulam, kaathiyakulam and vengadakulam. These clans are believed to be originated from four women born to a mother.

The settlement of the Mullukurumba are called *kudi* or *veedu* and a single house in a settlement is called *pera*. It is the smallest administrative, social and political unit of the Mullukurumba. For every *kudi,* there is a political head known as the *porunnon.* His jurisdiction constitute a settlement. *Porunnon* is assisted in his duties by another man called *porathon* (assistant). The position of *porunnon* is patrilineally inherited.

LIFE-CYCLE

Exogamy

Mullukurumba are strictly monogamous. In addition to that they practice tribal endogamy, clan exogamy and *veedu* (hamlet) exogamy. Close relatives are avoided in the selection of spouse. Ex-communication is given as punishment for violating the rules of exogamy. Cross-cousin marriages, marriage of boy with his own sister, and parallel cousin marriages are prohibited and consider illegitimate. Reciprocal marriages are also prohibited.

Bride-Price

The custom of bride-price still prevalent among the Mullukurumba and it is a compulsory compensation for the loss of economic contribution of a girl after her marriage. It is generally collected in various names such as (*a*) kaanapanam, (*b*) naattupanam, (*c*) parisappanam. *Kaanapanam* is a fixed amount worth rupees five and fifty paise. It is paid by the brother-in-law of the groom to the mother's brother of the bride, at the time of marriage. *Naattupanam* consists of only one rupee. Once this among is paid as charge for transfer of authority, the family has no authority or control over the girl. *Parisapanam* is not a fixed amount and it varies from 100 to 400 rupees depending on the financial status of the family usually paid before marriages.

Marriage Rituals

Among the Mullukurumba sagai (betrothal) ceremony is known as *pennukuri,* and marriage ceremony is called *kalyanama.* Generally marriages occur in the month of March, April and May because during these months they are economically improved after harvest. As per their belief Sunday, Wednesday and Thursday are considered auspicious for marriage.

Generally marriage proposals are made by the bridegroom's father. At first the groom's father visit the house of the concerned girl with a stick and bundle of betel leaves. He puts that bundle in front of their *daivapera* (sacred hut) and a ritual called *daivamkanal* is performed. It is a ritual of making obeisance to go. At his first time he does not reveal the purpose of his visit. But the people realise the intention of the visitor from the distribution of betel leaves to the hamlet members. In their vocabulary this man is called *pennookkaran.* After few days he comes again and discuss the matter with the bride's father to proceed to proposal. Next time bride's father again visit the groom's hamlet with his brother-in-law called by *moonammuthan* (middle man). This time marriage is fixed according to the convenience of both the parties. *Pennookkaran* and *moonammuthan* take *kanki* (gruel) with bride's father, maternal uncle of the bride and bride's brother.

Few days before marriage both bride's and groom's party performs a ritual called *daivamkanal* (making obeisance to god performed by the *velichapad* (oracle). Usually *parisapanam* is paid one week before marriage, and at that time betel leaves are also exchanged. This ritual is called *vettilakaimaral.*

Marriage usually takes place in the bride's hamlet. Before marriage the groom takes betel leaves from his mother's brother. The number of male persons are less in the groom's party, mostly five or six in addition to groom and his sister's husband. Groom's sister's husband is known as *kanamketty* because he carries the *kanappanam.* Groom's sister carries the bridal dress and she is called *mundukarathi* (mundu means cloth) the groom's party is called by *pennookkar.*

In the bride's hamlet, a bell metal lamp is placed in the centre of the *daivapera* (sacred hut where the marriage rituals take place and both the bride's groom's party stand at opposite sides. Groom's brother-in-law gives the *kaanapanam* to the mother's brother of the bride. It also includes a piece of gold called *puthumenupanam.* Groom's sister called *mundukarathi* places a cloth under it and the bridal dress. At that time groom's party are entertained with arecanut and betel leaves. Usually sacred thread or *thali* is tied to the bride by her maternal uncle on the previous day of marriage. So there is no such ceremony on marriage day, and marriage rituals are limited to giving of *kaanappanam* only.

Next major part of the ceremony is feast. It is served in the *daivapera* and the groom's party takes first. Groom and his relatives takes food along with the bride. Groom's brother-in-law washed the hands of the groom and groom's sister washes the hands of the bride. After the feast the bride goes to her groom's house. After reaching there, groom's mother take the bride to the *daivapera* and she is seated there. She is called *manavatti.* The close relatives put coins to the lap of this bride for which she returns betel leaves. A communal feast is also arranged there for the invitees. In the night the male people play *kolkkaly* (dance with a small stick called 'kol') and *vattakkali* (dance in a circular manner). Females also play *kolkkali* and *kaikottikkali.*

One day after marriage, the wife of the hamlet chief called *muthy* makes the bride grind paddy grain and also fetch water from the nearby river. It is a symbolic duty to denotes that the new in-law can accept the responsibilities of the groom's house. The new couple are invited to the bride's house for a feast after three days. They start with some close relatives and people from the bride's hamlet come in half way to invite them. This custom is called as *pathivazhivirunnu.* There is one more ritual known as *pittuvirunnu,* for that *dosai* (a flat white food item prepared with rice) are taken in two bundles from the groom's residence to the bride's settlement for distributing there. This is called *Marivirunnu.* The former is taking place on the third and the letter on the fifty day. This *dosai* exchange between the two houses is essential and it makes the completion of marriage ceremony.

While first visit to the bride's hamlet, the groom has to go for hunting customarily, along with the other men. If they got anything it is distributed in the hamlet. This custom is known as *manavalan nayattu* (*manavalan* means bridegroom and *nayattu* means hunt). The bride also has to do a similar ritual in the groom's hamlet that she has to go for fishing with other ladies of the settlement. This is known as *manavattymeenkoral* (*manavatty* means bride and *meenkoral* means fishing.

Mullukurumba have no speical dress at the time of marriage. The bridegroom use one white cloth in the waist upto knee, and another cloth is used to cover the upper portion of the body. A small piece of cloth is tied around the waist over the other one and it is called *manavalan kacha.* The bride use one white cloth over the lower part of the body (starting from waist and upto the knee) and another white piece of cloth is used to cover the chest and the two ends of this *mundu* are tied on the right shoulder, leaving the left shoulder free. This style is called *kettumundu.* In some cases another piece of white cloth called *pochumundu,* is also used to cover the shoulders, Mulluku rumba couple do not use any kind of special make-up at the time of marriage, except the application of turmeric powder in their body on the previous day of marriage.

A Mullukurumba bridegroom used to wear *kathala* (earring), *manavalan vala* (bangle), rigs... etc. After marriage *kathala* is changed and instead *kadukkan* (another ear ornament) is used. Kadukkan is the marriage symbol of the males. Rings are also used in the fingers.

Thali is the symbol of a woman's marital status given and tied by her mother's brother. At the time of marriage she also use *kathala,* rings, a silver armlet in the upper part of the elbow called *tholandi,* another bangle called *pattavala* or *manavatty vala* and *thappuvala. Thali* is also used in different types, *i.e. kuzhal thali, aelus, kunduthali, moortha thali...* etc.

The strict rule of endogamy obliges the Mullukurumba to marry within their own tribal group, and negotiated marriage is the accepted form of marriage. Marriages are solemnised after the attainment of puberty and monogamy is the socially recognised type. As like any other areas of traditions changes are also noticed in the area of Mullukurumba marriage. Now-a-days love marriages are common. Some of the families now want either to minimize their expenditure on marriage or to marry in simple form as they are economically poor. Educated youths expressed that they wanted to raise the age of marriage and they are selective in continuing the traditional customs.

Costumes

Now-a-day's traditional dress forms and ornaments are rarely seen in everyday life of the people, but in certain cases it is becoming a fashion and displayed at occasional celebrations and cultural festivals. Some of the items are even disappeared replacing the modern costumes. Actually traditional pattern of costumes identify a person to a particular cultural unit and most often highlights his or her position within that unit. More than the function of protection against diverse weather conditions, the costumes ensure a certain degree of modesty and affiliation to a group. Beyond all these, it is a symbolic representation of gender, status, designation and perspectives with some role of communication. This is true in the case of tribal communities. It is rare to find a tribe, which does not have its own characteristic styles and ceremonial costumes, which substantiate the understanding that costumes are culture specific.

The same is true in the case of ornaments and adornments. Body adornment is a universal channel of communication that not only serves to enhance individual attractiveness but also indicate the group's identity and origin. The interest towards ornaments and its materials differ from society to society. Starting from simple food gatherers to agricultural communities each group views with the rest to establish a sense of distinctiveness and the decorations and ornaments become more and more intricate. Here an attempt has been made to compare the dress and ornaments of three tribal communities of Kerala.

The communities Adiyan, Kattunaicken and Mullukuruman belong to economic categories such as food gatherers, agricultural labourers and settled agriculturists distributed in Wayanad district of Kerala. Now-a-days they are exposed to the neighboring cultures with different socio-cultural backgrounds, resulting changes in almost all aspects of their life and culture. Material culture is the most important element, subjected to different levels of advancements and variations due to technological improvements and new form of energy utilization. Even though these communities share the same ecosystem there are wide differences in their customs and practices along with other aspects of material culture including dress and ornaments.

ADIYAN

Male Costumes

Among Adiyan children below five years usually found nude and some of them are seen only in half trousers. Traditionally they use *konakam* (a piece of cloth tied to the waist covering the genital organs). Adult males wear single cloth called *mundu*. When they go out they wear a shirt called *kuppayam.* In addition to *kuppayam*, some of them also put a *thorthu* (towel) over the shoulder.

All married and unmarried men dress in the same style. The *mundu* is of cotton called *malmalmundu.* While doing work they use a *thorthumundu* (a towel which has a length up to knee).

Female Costumes

Females wear dark coloured saris called *chintae,* which is either black or red in colour. A knot is put on the shoulder with the two ends of the sari. This knot is called *chintakettu.* The arms and the left shoulder are left uncovered. Traditionally they did not use blouses. The length of the *chintae* extends up to the knee. A plain *thorthu* (towel) is used as underwear.

Married women can be distinguished from unmarried women in their knots on the sari. Spinsters have a single knot on their *chintae.* This is an identification to distinguish the married from the unmarried. While working, women keep the two ends of their sari in a single knot and are worn around in front of their cloth with a handle or cord. This is known as *cheerae.* In this bag they keep betel leaves, cash and ornaments.

Social and political functionaries generally put on a red cloth *pattu* around their waist. Traditionally Adiyan used ash for washing. Later it was replaced by soap nut called *cheenikaye.* Now-a-days Adiyan follow the dress pattern of their neighbouring non-tribes. Males use *mundu*, shirt, underwears, *lunki* (colour *mundu*), pants and other modern dresses. Likewise the females also use sari, blouse, underwear, *chooridar* and modern nightdresses. The number of pairs of dress depends upon the economic condition of the family. A major portion of their income is spent for buying dress, cosmetics, smoking and chewing tobacco and arecanut. Many of them are addicted to alcohol.

Ornaments

Traditionally young boys and girls wore no particular ornaments except a black thread around the neck. Girls wear a black thread around their waist also. After marriage male wears a silver bangle called *kaibala* and ear stud called *kadukku.* Girls above five years wear ear studs known as *kathala* or *olai* that are made of silver. *Olai* is also made of leaves of *pandanus*. They use a second ear stud called *miraves. Pandanus* leaves are dried mixing with ash and after rolling it is used as ear studs. Females also use nose studs called *mokubettu* and silver ranklets called *kalpavadam.* They put rings made of brass called as *chemmothira. Thali* or sacred thread is made of silver. There are three types of chains called *malakkallae, Karikkallae,* and *vellakkallae. Malakkallae* is a chain made of beads and stones. *Karikkallae* is a chain with silver coin as locket and *vellakkallae* is a chain or black thread with four *ana* (local measurement equal to 25 paise) coin as locket.

After marriage women wear two silver rings on their second toe, called *kalmothiram.* Women use glass bangles called *kuppibalai* and traditionally silver bangle was used on the upper arm called *tholbandhi* which is made of silver. Chief and other functionaries have a silver bangle *kadaga* that was usually given by the local landlord as the symbol of their designation. Women inherit a bead-bangle *kaimani* which is a material property inherited from mother to the daughter. Now-a-days woman wear ornaments made of cheap pearls and metals. They rarely use golden ornaments due to economic crisis.

MULLUKURUMBA

Male Costumes

Mullukurumba usually prefer white clothes. These white cotton clothes are known as *karikkanmundu.* Traditionally up to one year a baby is kept nude. At the age of five they are given a loincloth known as *konam,* and after that up to ten years a towel is used for covering the nudity. This towel is called *thorthu* approximately one and a half metre length, which extends up to knee. The *thorthu* used by an adult male is called *vellukambi.* Their traditional under-garment is known as *konam* which is same for both young and old people. After marriage a man usually puts another cloth on his shoulder known as *panthi* or *pochumundu.* This *pochumundu* on the shoulder and *thorthu* on the waist are the traditional dress of a mullukurumba male.

Female Costumes

Around the waist over the *mundu* the groom ties a band of multicoloured cloth known as *manavaln kacha.* The knot of the '*kacha*' is usually kept in front and its tip may reach up to the knee. On the occasion of marriage the bridegroom's dress pattern is different from that of others. Dress style on the occasion of marriage is known as *allimundu.* It is a long piece of white cloth torn in the middle and kept on the left shoulder, leaving the right shoulders free. The dead body is also dressed like that of the bridegroom.

A female child is also kept nude up to five years. As she grows a piece of cloth called *kettumundu* is used which wraps her body and tied on the left shoulder. Another piece of cloth called *araithuni* or *chuttukambi* is tied around the waist. This cloth worn inside the upper cloth serves the purpose of underwear. This is also known as *adimundu.* In addition to this another piece of cloth called *kachamuri* is tied to cover the breasts. It is wrapped around the body in a slanting position and the two ends of the cloth are tied on the left shoulder taking it below the right armpit. The right shoulder is kept uncovered. This cloth is known as *makkathi*. These three items of dress are used on the occasion of ceremonies connected with puberty ceremony. But the style of wearing *kettumundu* is different. Here it is tied across the chest just beneath the arms. The dress style of the bride differs from other ladies. A bride instead of tying a *kettumundu* on her shoulders, wraps herself with another *kachmuri,* covering the entire upper portion except face. This is known as *pochumundu.* The dead body of a female is also dressed like a bride as in the case of men.

Ornaments

Regarding the ornaments a black thread is tied round the waist of the newborn baby. After a few months (usually after ear boring ceremony) a small ear stud called *minni* is put on the ear. It is also known as *bandimullu,* which is made of gold or silver. In addition to this, *kaluvala* (anklets), *kaivala* (bangles), *nool* (waist band)... etc. are the ornaments worn by babies. This depends upon the economic capacity of the parents.

The ornaments are worn till the distinction of sex starts. Male children wear *kammal* (ear tops) or *kadukkan* (thick ear stud) and *aranjanam* (waist band). The ear ornament of adult male is known as *kathuminni.* Some of them wear this until marriage. At the time of marriage men wear an earring with a design called *kathala.* A silver bangle called *manavalan vala* was also used. In the past they continued to wear this even after marriage. In addition to this, three plain silver rings are also used during marriage. These silver rings are put in each fingers of the right hand except the thump and small finger. Around the waist they usually wear a silver thread known as *thodare* or *aranjanam.*

Girls put *kaivala* (bangles), *kammal* (ear stud), *malai* (beed necklace) and *mookuthi* (nose stud) until they get married. The ear ornament of an adult female is known as *kathumullu.* Usually at an age of ten years the girls bore their nose wings and put ornaments of silver called *bandhimullu.* At the age of thirteen or fourteen, *bandhimullu* is removed and wear ornaments known as *mukkuthi* or *mukkupotte.* Before marriage the females do noty wear any gold neck ornaments. Girls after puberty wear another type of necklace known as *panamala* or *kashumala* which gives the status of a girl who has attained puberty. After marriage a woman uses gold earning called *manikathala.* It is worn at the top of the ear, and below it another small oval shaped gold ring called *kathumara* is also used.

Some of these ornaments are not used for marriage. Instead, *kathala* (earring), *pattavala* (broad silver bangle), *chempadam* (silver anklet), *tholanki* (silver anklet)... etc. are used. Three silver rings are used in the fingers of the right hand except the thumb. In earlier days the married man and woman used to wear this ornament till his/her death. Marriage symbol is known as *moorthathali,* which is made of silver or gold depending on the economic capacity of the family. At the time of marriage the groom is accompanied by two social functionaries called *kanamketti* and *moonnaman.*

They also wear a white *mundu* (dothi). They simply wear a *panchimundu* over the shoulder. Both of the them use waistband over the *mundu.* The *kanamketti* wears a black *kacha* (cloth) and the *moonnaman* wears red *kacha.*

KATTUNAICKEN

Male Costumes

Traditionally the Kattunaicken males used to wear *mundu* or *seelae* (a long cloth) tied around the waist and extending up to the knees and a type of under-garment called *kachchae.* Some used *mel mundu* (upper cloth). *Soggeh* is the shirt worn by them. Now-a-days the younger generation wear brief, vest, pants and shirts.

Female Costumes

Females used to wear a long cloth called *chelae* (sari) in a particular style teaching just below the knees. This is also used to cover the upper portion of the body. The two ends of the *chelae* are tied on the left shoulder by taking it just below the right shoulders. Now they wear *lungi* (*mundu*) and *soggai* (blouse). They use the same dress when they go outside.

Ornaments

Traditionally kattunaicken women wear ornaments made of natural objects collecting from their surrounding ecosystem. They used to make a chain (bankara) with the stem of a plant known as *thai sappu*. Another type of grass called *saya hollu* (oil grass) is used to prepare bangles (*valai*). Here also the stem is taken and dried. It is then split and twisted. Both ends are tied to form a circle and are used as a bangle. They also prepare finger rings in the same manner. Kattunaicken used a particular type of nose stud made of thorns called *karamullu* and *kattumullu.* These thorns are collecting from the forest. Now-a-days younger generation used to wear nose studs made of gold or silver. Females used to put ear studs called *ola* made of silver. They also wore nose studs called *mukubettu.* Necklace called *kallumalai* made of locally available pearls and they generally use shining stones. There are three types of bangles called *bandhi, bala* and *gadaga* worn by women. *Bandhi* is made of silver, *balai* and *gadaga* are with bronze. Kattunaicken women also use silver anklets called *kalapilli* and rings called *unkara.* Tattooing is known as *asile.* They usually do it.

Traditional leaders like moopan used to wear a particular type of bangle called *cheesa valai* made of silver. Some times these bangles are converted to a flat structure and miniatures of this were used as ear stud called *kadukka.* They believed that with this ear stud, the evil forces would not touch them. Today men use *chooral* (a kind of reed bamboo) for making ear stud instead of other type of ornaments. Females put small pieces of the mid rib of coconut leaf called *irkkil* as ear stud and nose stud.

The tribal groups such as the Kattunaicken, the Adiyan and the Mullukurumba have an intimate relationship with their ecosystem. They have been interacting with the ecosystem since thousands of years, and thus their interaction with the environment has been successful mainly because the surroundings provided them food, shelter, and livelihood strategies.

When go through the dress and ornaments of Kattunaicken, Adiyan and Mullukurumba, it is seen that the emblems of allegiance are closely related to their traditional mode of living and interaction with the ecosystem. As a food gathering society, Kattunaicken uses very simple pattern of ornaments and these are mostly prepared with the items collected from the forest. The dress and ornaments of Adiyan also shows simple pattern. As agricultural labourers they struggle hard to two ends meet and their income is not sufficient to buy costly items of dress and ornaments. The situation of Mullukuruman is better than Kattunaicken and Adiyan. As they are settled agriculturists they are in a better economic condition to buy things. More over the townships and the provision centre that grew supplied commodities or consumer items to the tribes. A society whose culture is determined by economy, changes first happen in their material culture especially dress, ornaments and household equipments. The economic transformation is one of the most important factors that have contributed to changes in material culture.

REFERENCES

1. Luiz, A.A.D., 1962, *The Tribes of Kerala,* New Delhi: Bharatiya Adimjati Sevak Sang.
2. Mathur, P.R.G., 1977. *Tribal Situation in Kerala,* Trivandrum: Kerala Historical Society.
3. Mann, R.S. and Mann, K., 1989. *Tribal Culture and Change,* New Delhi: Mittal Publications.
4. Rapoport, Amos, 1982. *The Meaning of the Built Environment: A Non-verbal Communication Approach,* Beverly Hills: Sage
5. Bindu, B., 1990. 'Settlement pattern and house types among the Mullukurumba "(unpublished M.A. dissertation submitted to Calicut University).
6. Bindu, B., 1998 "Socio-economic change among three Wayanad tribes—A study of Kattunaicken, Adiyan and Mullukurumba in eco-cultural context" (Unpublished Ph.D. thesis submitted to Calicut university).

CHAPTER 2

Baiga

Dr. Prakash Chandra Mehta

The earliest account of the Baiga that has come down to us as recent as 1867, when captain Thomson, in his Seoni Settlement Report, briefly described them as 'the wildest of the tribes, inhabiting the most inaccessible hills and the remotest forests: living on what they can secure with their bows and arrows, in the use of which they are very skilful, and on the forest produce, and on the small crops which they grow on the hill sides. They are extraordinarily shy, so that it is often difficult to get hold of them, unless you are accompanied by someone the knew. They fly out at one end of the village as you appear at the other, and you can see them scrambling up the hill side amongst the stones and bushes, or holding and peeping at you from behind the bushes like wild animals."

Colonel Ward as the first to investigate the life and habits of the tribe in any detail, and he has some interesting pages on the subject in his Mandala Settlement Report, published in 1870. He seems to have found the Baiga a great deal easier to get hold of, and soon had them eating with him, and even offering him wives. 'Wild as the forest they live in ... they are independent, high spirited ... very well behaved, ready to oblige, and deserving every consideration for their orderly manner at life. Conspicuous for their absence of dress, they live in much better huts, and more orderly villages, than their namesakes (near Mandla).

About this time Forsythis classical highlands of central India appeared. He too was greatly taken by the Baiza. Far superior to the Gods in every respect, he says are the still utterly unreclaimed forest Baigas. A few of these have somewhat modified their original habits, and live, along with the goods, in the villages lower down the valleys. These have been slightly tainted with Hinduism, shave their elfin locks, and call themselves by a name denoting caste. But the real Baiga of the hill ranges is still almost in a state of nature.

Origin

The Baiga appear to be a branch of the Bhuiya tribe, which still numbers half a million in Bengal and Bihar, and is to be found chiefly in Madhya Pradesh of Jashpur and Serguja. The Bhuiya who are also called Bhumia, are as their name implies, lords of the soil. This title is also claimed by the Baiga who call themselves Bhumiaraja or Bhumijan, and Bhumia is name given to the most important sub-section of this tribe.

The Baiga tribe of the central provinces are really a branch of the Bhulya. Though the Baigs are now mainly returned from Mandla and Balaghat, it seems likely that there districts were not their original home, and that they emigrated from Chhattisgarh into the Satpura hills on the western borders of the plain. The hill country of Mandla and Maikal range of Balaghat from one of the widest and most inhospitable tracts in the province, and it is unlikely that the Baigas would have made their first settlements here and spread thence into the fertile plain of Chhattisgarh. Migration in the opposite direction would be more natural and probable. But it is fairly certain that the Baiga tribe were among the earliest if not the earliest residents of the Chhattisgarh plain and the hills north and east of it. The Bhaina, Bhunjia and Binjhwar tribes who still reside in this country all be recognized as offshoots of Baigas. Some of the oldest forts in Bilaspur are attributed to the Bhainas and a chief of this tribe is as having ruled in Bilaigarh south of Mahanadi. They are said to have been dominant in Pendra where they are still most numerous, and to have been expelled from Phuljhar in Raipur by the Gonds. The Binjhwars or Binjals again are an aristocratic sub-division of Baigas, belonging to the hills east of Chhattisgarh and the Uriya plain country of Sambalpur beyond them. The zemindars of Bodasamar, Rampur, Bhatgaon and other estates to the south and east of the Chhattisgarh plain are members of this tribe. Both the Bhainas and Bijhwars are frequently employed as priests of the village deities all over the area and may therefore be considered as older residents than the Gond and Kawar tribes. Sir G. Grierson also states that the language of the Baigas of Mandla and Balaghat is a form of Chhattisgarhi, and thus is fairly conclusive evidence of their first having belonged to Chhattisgarh. Sir H. Risley claimed that the Binjhlas or Binjhwars of Chota Nagpur are their ancestors came from Ratanpur twenty generations ago.

Russel goes on to argue that the Chhattisgarh plain and the hills north and east of it belong to the same tract of the country as the Chota Nagpur states which are the home of the Bhuiya. There is thus no geographical difficulty in supposing the Baiga to be a branch of this tribe.

Again, the name Baiga means a sorcer or medicine man. It is applied in this sense to the priests of the Chota Nagpur tribe, the Kairwar. The Bhuiyar of Mirzapur, who seem to be identical with the Bhuiya of Chota Nagpur, are also called Baiga in so far as they perform the function of propitiating the local and ancient deities as their priests. The name Baiga is also applied in the Central Provinces to anyone who serves as a village priest–the Pardhan, the Ghasiya, the Karwar, and Gond and many Hindu castes use the word in this sense.

The Baigas of Mandla are also known as Bhumia, which is only a variant of Bhiya, having the same meaning of lords of the soil or belonging to the soil. Both Bhuiya and Bhumia are in fact nearly equivalent to our word "aboriginal", and both the names are to the tribe by the Hindus and not originally that by which its members called themselves. It would be quite natural that a braner of the Bhuiyas, who settled in the Central Provinces and were commonly employed as village priests by the Hindus and Gonds should have adopted the name of the office, Baiga, as their tribal designation; just as the title of Munda or village headman as become the name of one branch of the Kol tribe, and Bhumij, another term equivalent to Bhuiya of a second branch.

It can be said that Baiga belongs to Munda or Kolarian tribe. What little evidence we have, moreover, suggests that the Baiga represent the earliest settlement of all; their Kol and Gond neighbours regard them as priests knowing the original secrets of the local soil; they accept their decisions on boundary disputes. Colonel Ward found the help of the Baiga invaluable when he was making his settlement; and they look up to them as an older race. It can be accepted that there were two separate settlements of Kolarian and Munda race, the first represented by the Bhar, Bhuiya, Baiga and kindered tribes who have entirely lost their own languages and have names given to them by the Hindus, and the second represented by the Kol or Munda and their related tribes.

The word 'Kolarian', of course, is not properly applied to an ethnic unit. The term, however, is convenient and familiar, and Baron von Elkstedt's new classification, interesting as it is, has yet won universal acceptance. He himself appears to class Baiga as 'Gondid', but this is surely a slip, the Baiga are obviously distinct from the Gond and should be placed in the 'Kolid' group.

Clan

The primary allegiance of every Baiga, whatever his sub-caste may be, is to the Baiga tribe itself. The tribe is strictly endogamous, although as we see, women of other tribes who marry Baiga may be admitted after the appropriate rites have been performed.

The Baiga tribe is divided into a number of more or less endogamous, because the rules about intermarriage vary from place to place.

Colonel Ward was the first to give a list of three sects or castes of Baiga viz. Binjwar or Binehwar, Mondya and Bherontha. Colonel Bloomfield, writing of Balaghat, also knew of only three–the Narotia, Bharotia and Binjhwar. Russell gives the names of seven clans viz. Binjhwar, Bharotia, Narotia or Nahar, Raibhaina, Kathabhaina, Kondwan or Kundi and Gondwaina. Today we must add to the list Kurka Baiga, Sawat Baiga and Dudh-Bhaina. The subsections have probably arises from inter-marriage with other tribes or perhaps a leading member of a group of villages have committed some tribal offence and have been supported by the fellow villages with the result that they have been expelled from the main stock and taken a new name. The Chhota Bhumia of Niwas came into existence by this way. They are Bhumia who clean themselves with water instead of leaves, and dress in Gond fashion, so that the other Bhmia refuse to eat with them.

The main clans of Baiga we can see today are Bharotia, Binjhwar, Bhumia, Muria, Bhaina, Dudh-Bhaina, Kath-bhaina, Rai-bhaina, Kondwan Baiga, etc. are the important class of this tribal group.

Costumes

The clothes and ornaments of the Baiga have no special significance, for they neither spin nor weave, but buy their clothes from the local *Panka* or *Mehra* who weave cloth with mill-made yarn, and their ornaments from the local market.

Male Costumes

The orthodox Baiga tradition is to wear as little as possible. The man put on a very small *dhoti,* often it is only a *langoti* with a broad flap which hangs down in front. This is sometimes made of the some pink-coloured cloth as the woman's *lugra.* In the cold, they tie a thick double cloth, the *kapchi*, round their shoulders. On the head they wear a rag called *patka* or *pharria*, but some of the rich Baiga use turban of twenty hands long. Some, but very few, wear rather elaborate sandals called *bhadai* or country shoes, but the majority go unshod. Boys wear a *bharria* rag round their loins.

The Muria Baiga wear a small cloth round the loins but without the flap in front, after the Gond custom. The Binjhwar dress is more or less nearer to Hindu fashion viz. *dhoti,* shirt, coat or waistcout, and wear the small round cap, the bamboo lining of which they make themselves.

Female Costumes

Bhumia women wear a long strip of cloth called *chitra* or *lugra* tied round the waist, carried up across the breasts, over the right shoulder, and tucked in at the back. The skirt thus formed is often very short, not reaching to the knees. The head is left bare. Bharotia and Narotia women also wear *lugra* like this but Binjhwar and few Muria cover themselves up a bit more, wearing the *lugra* over both shoulders, some times over the head, and they tie the *kanch* in the Gond fashion.

The wearing of the *kanch* is most generally difference between various section of Baigas. To wear the *kanch* that one end of the *lugra* is brought down between the legs and tucked firmly in at the waist. It is tied very strongly. It is in fact worn something like a man's *dhoti*. The other method is to tie it like a skirt. The Baiga wear the *kanch* wherever Gond influence is strong. It is not a specially Hindu custom.

Bhumia women do not wear the *choli* or bodice, but in some are a they wear jacket called *jhulawa.* During the menstrual period they wear a small strip of cloth called *chindhi* between the legs. It is tucked in at either end through the *kardhan* (relic of the old leaf-dress), the cord that is always worn about the waist, and is thus held in place.

Young girls, wear a *lugri,* a small strip of cloth tied skirt-wise round the waist. After puberty, they throw the end of the *lugri* over the right shoulder. This is the *Khandela,* and the girl is called *khandlahin,* she is mature.

Ornaments

Both the sexes are very much fond of ornaments. Men wear iron or silver bracelets, one on each wrist called *chura.* On the third little fingers of either hand they wear a *mundri* (ring) of brass, aluminimum, silver, copper or gold. In the ears, they wear the *bari* in the upper part, the *bala* in a hole through the middle, and the *lurki* through the lobe. The *bari* made of blue and white beads strung on a circle of fine wire. The *bala* is very similar but larger in size. The *lurki* is a small ring of gold or silver.

The old men do not use ornaments, others dress up for festivals. Generally man wears only an iron *sankri,* or chain, in which they believe that deity resides. Yogi wears a necklace of black and read beads.

At dance the men wear a *kalngi* of *peacock's* feathers struck in the turban, and *chhuta,* a necklace of gray-coloured beads, round the neck. On their feet they wear *paijna* anklets with little beads. Sometimes they wear the *chhit,* a red cloth tied round the head like a turban, and a special shirt called *jhanga.* Some wear a *neur* made of peacocks' feathers on the chest and back. The young men may wear almost anything at a glance. They may put on any ornament they can easily find; the *hawel* is very popular among them.

Bhumia women wear the *dhar,* but without its characteristic chains. In the same hole in the lobe of the ear in which the *dhar* is worn, they also wear the *pola,* a thick round bit of wood, with a hole through the middle, which keeps the aperture open when other ornaments are not used. The *pola* may be made of leaves, the thin stock of *tuma* gourd, or the stalic of maize. The *tarki* is a similar ornament but is fixed with lac. The Baiga women sometimes wear the brass umbrella-shaped *kinwa* in their ears. To take these ornaments, the hole in the ear is very slowly enlarged. First, a single bit of grass is inserted, then another and another. The little bundle may go on growing from three months to a year.

The Baiga women do not use nose-ornaments. This is an important rule distinguishing them from other tribe. For tying the hair they use woollen *phundara* or sometimes the silk *jhela,* very rarely they wear a silver *mangchirni* across the head in the manner of the Gond *bindia.*

In the neck they wear *chhuta,* a necklace of coloured beads, other neck ornament is *suita* which is tight round the neck is made of silver, other ornaments are *hawel*—a necklace of silver coins, *Kanthi*—of black beads, *Latkania* of read, blue and yellow beads and *guria bichuli*—a series of coloured squares are popular among them.

They use to wear *mundri* on the fingers and *chura* or *patta* on the wrist. On the feet, *chura* are also worn: these are called *tin-kor* they are heavy brass anklets with wide rings. They also wear brass or silver anklets down over the heel, they have *gheengru* or little bits of metal inside to make them tinckle. On the toes they use *chutki,* and a big *chutka* on the big toe.

Different sections of Baiga may easily be distinguished by the ornaments. The Bhumia wear least of all for though the above, they rarely wear more than one or two of them. Only the Bhumia generally use the heavy brass *tin-kor* round the ankles. The Bharotia are distinguished by wearing only brass bangles, a lot of them; the highest upto the arm, bigger than others, is called the *darkna.* The others are *kaknahi.* They do not use *tarki* or any ornament faced with lac.

For protection from the rain, a wicker hood lined with mohlain leaves, the *khumra* or *khumri,* is worn over the head, and a rough 'beanket is tied across the shoulders with a big knot just below the chin. In the rains they also wear a wooden cloge knows as *kharaut.*

For carrying money or tobacco, the Baiga use a number of little bags. Women wear the small knitted *gupti* round their neck. Men also use the *gupti,* but the long knitted *basni* tied round the waist is very popular. The *thali* is another kind of bag for money is made of woven cloth or sambhar skin.

Tattooing

Baigas are very much fond of tattooing. Women themselves take a great pride in their tattoo-marks. The usual marks tattooed on a Baiga woman are a triangular decoration is made on the forehead when a Baiga girl is about five year old. On the breast is a peacock, or a *dauri* (basket) and on the arm the *haldi-ganth* (the turmeric root). These are marked or tattooed when the girl reaches puberty. At the time of marriage or later, a *jhophari* (a pattern of any kind) is tattooed on the back of the hand, the lines of dots known as *palani* or *kajeri* on the things, and in between *palani* the bail *ankhi,* on the knee is the *phulia,* round like a flower, and on the back are flies and many other types of mark are tattooed on the body parts.

Men are seldom tattooed, but they sometimes tattooed *chandrama* (moon) on the back of the hand and the *bichhu* (scorpion) on the fore-arm. Sometimes they tattoo themselves on the affected parts in order to cure rheumatism.

Hence like other tribals of the country their dress and ornaments are different from other tribal groups of the country which gives them specific identity which reflects their rich cultural heritage.

CHAPTER 3

Bhil

Dr. (Mrs.) Sonu Mehta

In the tribal heritage of India, the Bhils have a special identity and substantial contribution. They constitute about one crore population which is about 15 per cent of the total tribal population of India. Bhils stand third in population after Santhals and Gonds. The concentration of Bhils in the country can be observed in four states viz. Rajasthan, Gujarat, Maharashtra and Madhya Pradesh, while they can also be seen in the southern and eastern part of the country i.e. Andhra Pradesh, Karnataka and Tripura.

Bhil is the second largest tribal group of the state of Rajasthan after the Minas and constitute more than 40 per cent of the tribal population. According to 1991 census the Bhils were 2,305,982 (1,177,865 males and 1,128,117). They can be seen throughout the Rajasthan, their concentration is in southern part of the state viz. Banswara, Dungarpur and Udaipur districts having more than 50 per cent of the Bhils. This area also have been included in the Tribal Sub Plan Area (TSP) of the State for special development of the tribal groups.

Origin

The Bhils are recognised as the oldest living inhabitants of the country. Anthropologists and sociologists, for more than a century have been trying to find out their origin. But they are not able to conclude any unanimous opinion about their origin. It is certainly said that they are aboriginals of this country and residing in remote and dense forest since long.

The word 'Bhil' is the deform of 'Bhill' of Sanskrit language. This is originally related to *Bhil-Bip-Bhadne* (भील बिल भेदने). In Sanskrit the word Bhill is used for non-aryans. In Sanskrit word Bhill mean to interact or pierce (*Bhedna*). Robert Shefer had tried to establish *Nishad* the ancestor of Bhils. According to him the Bhils are origin "Nishad-Madhav". In this reference he quoted the *"Vajsanchi Sanhita"* of mahidhar. It is also believed that this word Bhil or Bhill has been used upto 600 A.D. before that they were perhaps called by the names of *Pulind* & *Vanputra* etc.

Bhils have several legends regarding their origin.

History

Very little is known about the early Bhils. The historical records available upto the end of 7th century does not give us appreciable accounts about the history, culture and life of the Bhils until about 626 A.D. The Bhill having a glorious past in the history and earned good name. They have established relations with the then rulers. In few states they were rulers and established the states on their own names viz. Dungarpur on *Dungria Bhil.* Kushalgarh on *Kushla,* Kota on *Kotiya* Bhill etc. Due to their relations with the *Rajput* rulers, they established good or bad relations with the then rulers. They have put a loss with their good relations and in some cases they rushed back to the dense forests. Hence in the history, the Bhils have seen good times or co-ordial relations with the rulers on the other hand from time to time they faced bad events or ill-relations with the rulers. So throughout the history they had been in the light. During the Maratha and British period Bhils have seen very bad time and extremely exploited by them.

Inhabitation

The Bhils today observe the age-old settlement pattern of scattered inhabitation. In this pattern each house is away from other house and fields are surrounded by their hutments. The scattered pattern of settlement have a special feature of vigilance i.e. on the crop as well as animals. Bhils always like to settle outside the village or, far away from the village, they do not like to live within the village.

The age-old *Pal* settlement also exists. *Pal* is an endogamous. Generally *Pals* having 10 to 15 families and a number of *Pal* constitute a village.

The Bhils prefer nuclear family, so they live in a single hut which serves as a multipurpose room for them. Their hut also have a *Varanda* and a courtyard or fencing of plants. In the fencing, they tie their live-stock like bullock, cow, goat etc. After marriage of their son, they construct another hut for this new couple. Such sort of fragmentation of family carries out till the marriage of last or youngest son.

Clan

Every society have clans. Clan system is very important in settling the marriage relations. The clan system plays an important role in the *Pal* and *Villages* i.e. in a *Pal* or village persons reside in them belong to single clan or two-three clans. Hence the Bhils observe clan system very seriously.

Bhils are organized into a number of patrilineal exogamous groups or clans locally known as *Atak* that rests on the "fiction of common decent from a founding ancestor who lived so far the distant past as to be a mythological"....?. Each clan distinctively named, consists of the totality to related individuals from the same ancestors. Each clan has its own *totem*. The *totem* may be a plant, bird or animal. All clan members invoke their respective *totemic* gods and goddesses locally known as *Devta*. During their hard times and difficulties or on the special occasion they perform ceremony. They also observe the ranking of clan i.e. lower and upper group.

The prevalent clans in the Bhils are viz. Angari, Ahari, Uthed, Kaluva, Kalasua, Koted, Dabi, Damor, Dindor, Rot, Solanki, Bhagora, Rathore etc. The number of clans are increasing day-to-day and throughout the Bhil region.

Family

The Bhils like nuclear family in which husband, wife and their unmarried children live together. They do not prefer joint family, as can be seen in Hindus. When a grown up son marries, he separates from his parents and establishes new family. For establishing new couple, the father construct another hut for him and give a part of a land for his survival and by this way fragmentation carried out till all his sons married. The head of family is father or the oldest male member of family in the absence of father in Bhil family. The parents generally live together with youngest son. This sort of family system can be seen throughout the Bhil region.

Life-Cycle

Birth Rituals: Generally Bhil couple like the child. Every couple wishes that they must have a child whether it may be male or female i.e. boy or girl. In Bhil society no difference have been observed in male and female child, both are given equal importance. During pregnancy of women, Bhils do not observe any ceremony. After the delivery they celebrate it. Usually on the birth of son they beat *thali* (metal plate) and on the birth of girl they beat *sup* (winnowing fan). They observe purification ceremony after 5 to 7 days of birth of child. On this day the mother and child take bath and *Suraj Pujan* ceremony is observed for the welfare of child and mother. On this day a feast is also arranged and songs also sung by ladies. The nearer relatives give presents to the mother and child. During the delivery period they try to feed the mother well and give her nourishing diet whatever they can afford. The Bhils also observe naming and *Mundan* ceremonies.

Marriage: Marriage among the Bhils is not a sacrament. Like the Hindu marriage it is not indissolvable. In Bhil society child marriage is not prevalent. For a Bhil, both male and female marriage is a mark of adulthood and maturity.

In Bhil society different forms of marriages are prevalent among them. They prefer marriage by elopement and traditional marriage which is performed by full rituals by the parents of girl and boy. The prevailing marriages are (1) Marriage by tradition *(Morbandhiya Vivah)* (2) Marriage by elopement (3) Marriage by trial *(Pariviksha Vivah)* (4) Marriage by purchase (5) Marriage by service *(Seva Vivah).* (6) Marriage by exchange (7) Marriage by consent (8) Marriage by rigidness *(Huth Vivah)* and (9) *Natra* Marriage.

In *Traditional Marriage* all the ceremonies are performed right from *Sagai* to *Vidai* in the house of boy and girl. But the criteria for the marriage is bride price locally known as *dapa.* Before *Sagai,* bride price is settled between the girl and boy's father, if any dispute arises the matter has to be decided by the *Patel* of both sides. In this sort of marriage all rituals are performed according to Hindu marriage.

Widow marriage is prevalent among the Bhil society. It is performed in simple manner. Generally, among Bhils, the marriage with the deceased elder brother's wife, called *Devar Vattor* marriage is prevalent. This marriage does not carry any elaborate rituals at its celebration. In case the deceased husband has no brother or she do not wish to marry with him, the widow is married to some one else. In this case the bride-price is charged by the widow's father. The Bhil widow marry after the mourning period.

Divorce in the Bhils can be seen in exceptional cases, but *Nata* marriage is prevalent among the Bhils. The main criteria for the *Nata* is *dapa*. In this case the *dapa* is known as *Jagdha* and the woman is known as *Jhagde ki Aurat*.

***Death*:** In Bhils the dead bodies are cremated except in case of those who die in infancy, snake bite or due to some epidemic, the dead body is burried. Bhils observes all the rituals which are performed by the caste *Hindus* on the occasion of death. They observe 13 days mourning and arrange feast on the 13th day.

Costumes

Costume adorns the body and enriches its appearance, making a person gorgeous and enchanting besides safeguarding his/her body. Thus costume not only serves the utilitarian purpose of covering the body but also used with special effect to enhance the beauty and elegance of the person.

Whatever, might be the origin of the costume it provides the visible index of the homogeneity and the unity of people. Costume conveys more than mere clothing. It also includes: coiffure and ornaments. Coiffure refers to headdress and hairstyle while ornaments are used for decoration of the body parts–it includes jewellery, tattooing, body painting, etc.

Costume has been functioning as a fashioner of personality and has tended to be cultivated as an art in today's world. As every community has its unique way to dressing which at a glance distinguish it from the other communities, for example, Rajasthani women wear *odhni, ghaghra* and *Choli*, while Punjabi women wear *Salwar-Kurta* and *Dupatta*. Similarly Bhil tribe also has its unique costume which distinguish them from other tribal groups.

Kotra Panchayat Samiti regarded as the most remote, wild and dangerous of all panchayat samities of Udaipur: dangerous because of (*i*) The presence of leopards, bears and pythons in its jungle, although tigers are now rarely seen and (*ii*) The lawlessness of local inhabitants, who regarded travellers as their customary prey.

It is only during the last 15 years that the resources of its forests have begun to by systematically explored. A road was also constructed between Kotra and Udaipur.

This link of Kotra Udaipur brings many changes in the lifestyle of Bhil residing there. Previously it is said that the tribeman would never bring any change in their living. These people believe that god would punish them if they bring and change in their living.

But with the passing of time a new invention emerge in the horizon, changes are seen in all the phases of life. The effect of changing devices on Bhils society could not be saved, they have also joined steadily the mainstream of national life. Now we can see the effect of changing face in the Bhil culture, in the vastness of culture matrix, some of the elements are still remain untouched, one most significant elements among this is costume which is one of the three basic needs of human being i.e. food, clothing and shelter. The details of the garments and ornaments such as fabric, designs, pattern of garment, metal used in jewellery, motifs of lockets and tattooing etc. are still not known.

Seeing all these factors there arises a need to study the very distinctive traditional apparel, jewellery, footwear and other accessories of Bhil tribe which is densely populated in Kotra Panchayat Samiti of Udaipur district.

During the field visit I have personally observed these folks in Kotra Panchayat Samiti of Udaipur district in distinctive dresses and jewellery which created an interest to conceptualize the traditional and changing trends in each of the garment of Bhil tribe, fabrics used, design prevalent, pattern of the garment, jewellery, hairstyle, tattooing and footwear. The details of jewellery worn on different body parts of females is discussed in appendix.

Thus in order to explore the Bhil costume, coiffiene and ornaments the study was conducted in kotra Panchayat Samiti of Udaipur district (Udaipur stands, second in the concentration of Bhil population in Rajasthan) on 120 respondents of different age groups from 4 villages.

The major findings of the study are:

1. The traditional Bhil female costume was *Kanchli, gherdar Ghaghra* and *Odhni* (1 M by 1.5 M.)
2. The traditional Bhil male costume was *Dhoti, Kurta* and *Pagadi*.
3. The changes found in the Bhil female costumes from last 1 decade, mainly because of mobilisation and interaction to the urban community.
   (*a*) The preference for *Kanchli* was reducing day by day and the inclination towards the blouse was increasing.
   (*b*) The change was also found in the dimensions of the *Odhni*: The larger dimension of *Odhni* (1.5 M by 2.5 M) was more prevalent than traditional i.e. smaller demension (1 M by 1.5 M).
   (*c*) The traditional *gherdar Ghaghra* was taken over by the pleated and petticot *ghaghra*.
4. The change that had occurred in the Bhil male costumes was that shirt and pant had been adopted

from last 2 decades. Regarding headdress it was observed that those respondents who wore pant- shirt did not wear any headdress.

5. The presence of synthetic fabric was recognised in the Bhil market from last one decade only. Prior to this only cotton was used, but with the emergence of synthetic fabric the preference for synthetic was increased and today most of the Bhils prefer synthetic fabric.
6. Both Bhil males and females were fond of wearing different ornaments on different body parts. Silver was the only metal used in jewellery. The Bhil females generally wore all the jewellery they possess, the most common were *dhimna, long, ognia, hasali, tagli, viti, kada, kakona, anwala, pajeb, bichhudi*, etc. while the males generally wore silver *buttons, sankhali, viti kada, murki* etc. Traditionally *Pinjaini* was the main ornament worn by the females but now it had been totally replaced by *kada, pajeb, anwale* and other leg ornaments.
7. The tattooing was the commonly preferred body decoration from last 4 decades till today. The only change observed was in the amount of tottooing, traditionally it was done on face, legs, neck and full hand but today only one or two designs were made on the hand and face.
8. For the improvement in appearance the various cosmetic materials were used by young Bhil males and females from last one decade. But prior to this no cosmetics were used by these people.
9. Some of the Bhils remain bare footed traditionally, but now every person wear either rubber chapple, plastic shoes or leadher *Mojadia* as foot wear.
10. The change was occurred in the concept of Bhils regarding the selection of garments for children. As

they use frock, skirt, toppers for girl child and for boys nickker and shirts.

Thus it can be concluded that the Bhils have rich heritage in their traditional costume, coiffence and ornaments and the older generation is still included towards these however the gradual changes in their costume can be observed from last one decade. These changes are mainly due to their increased interaction and mobilization towards urban areas. As they move out for wages and came in contact with various visual and audio aids which directly or indirectly influence their style of living.

Jewellery worn on different body parts by females

Sl. No.	Body Part	Name of Jewellery	Weight of Jewellery
1.	Head	Bor	10-15 gm
		Borla	20-30 gm
		Jhela	80-100 gm
2.	Nose	Long	5-10 gm
		Nath	10-15 gm
		Bhavariya	10-15 gm
3.	Ear	Dhimma	
		Oganiya	
		Jumar	
4.	Neck	Hasali	1-1.5 kg
		Sakhali	1-1.5 Kg
		Madalia	30-40 gm
		Tagli	.5 to 1.5 kg
5.	Hand	Bhujband	60-70 gm
		Kakona	70-100 gm
		Tadiyan	60-80 gm
		Gajara	40-60 gm

Sl. No.	Body Part	Name of Jewellery	Weight of Jewellery
		Kada	100-300 gm
		Chelkada	100-300 gm
6.	Finger	Viti	5-15 gm
		Hathful	8-120 gm
7.	Waist	Kandora	600-800 gm
		Judo	80-100 gm
8.	Ankle	Kadala	300-500 gm
		Anwale	70-80 gm
		Pajeb	100-150 gm
		Thankle ghughre	80-100 gm
9.	Toes	Bhichhia	5-30 gm

CHAPTER 4

Damor

Dr. Prakash Chandra Mehta

The Damor is a small tribal group, migrated from Gujarat state and are largely located in the Simalwara Block of Dungarpur district of Rajasthan adjoining to Gujarat state. The Damors have a population of 43,612 persons (21,801 males and 21,811 females) according to 1991 census.

The Damors of the border of Gujarat and Rajasthan in the district of Dungarpur speak Gujarati of mixed form. A majority of them speak Vagri which is local dialect spoken by rest of the population of Dungapur district.

The Damor are taken to be a branch of the Bhils. The identity of Damors is largely due to habitation and forming interior villages on hills bordering Gujarat from where they migrated. Damor in the state of Rajasthan have been declared as scheduled tribe but not so in Gujarat state.

Damor consider themselves superior to the Bhils. There are some chances that some Rajputs might have married Bhil girls whose progeny would have demarcated a separate identity like Damors.

Damors also called Damarias and have no sub-groups. In Rajasthan they are declared in the list of scheduled tribe, while in Gujarat they are covered under general category.

Damors have two clans–one upper Damor and other lower Damor. Both groups treat themselves superior, but marital relations are restricted between them. Both the groups are exogamous and have their own clans.

Most of the clans have similarity with Rajput clans. They believe that their ancestors were Rajputs and due to some social sin they were debarred from the caste and fallen into group of tribals.

Family

Damors prefer nuclear family in which father, mother and unmarried sons and daughters live together. Generally parents prefer to live with their youngest married son. Joint family is rare. They are patrilineal and patrilocal.

Lifecycle

***Birth Rituals*:** In the Damors first delivery generally takes place in the house of girl's parents. The succeeding deliveries take place in the house of parents or at their own house. An elderly women of the family acts as midwife. Usually the period of confinement is limited to twelve days after the delivery. On the twelfth day the mother worships the sun with her relative and neighbours known as *'Suraj Puja'*. Sister of the husband has specific role to play after the birth of the child.

The Damors invite Brahmin to perform the *Namkaran* ceremony. This ceremony is performed after the third or fourth month of the birth of the child. The role of the *Bhuwa* is important in the name giving. Damor usually name the child on the basis of week days or after ancestors or *totems*.

Like high caste Hindus *mundan* ceremony is observed among the Damors. Generally the *Bhuwa* accepts the hair of the new born. In this ceremony *Bhuwa* presents cloths to the infant. Such presents are also given by relatives.

When there is no male child in the family, a husband may either be permitted to marry another women or to adopt brother's or sister's son. Sometimes son-in-laws can also be accepted as successor.

***Marriage Rituals*:** The marriage age varies between 12 to 15 years, both in case of male and female. The negative checks are clan exogamy. *Sapinda* restriction i.e. there is no preference for cross cousin or parallel cousin marriage, they can not marry out of Damor tribe and a boy can marry a Bhagat or non-Bhagat Damor irrespective of his category of orientation, *Dapa* or brideprice has to be paid for marriage.

Polygamy does not exists in this tribal group, but exceptions can be seen. Pre-marital relations are not permitted in the society. In case of deviation of this rule, the offenders have been punished. The proposal for marriage is initiated by the parents of the boys. The instances of marriage by elopement can be seen. Generally marriage is performed by a Brahmin priest on Hindu pattern. Usually, after marriage the spouses live in a separate house.

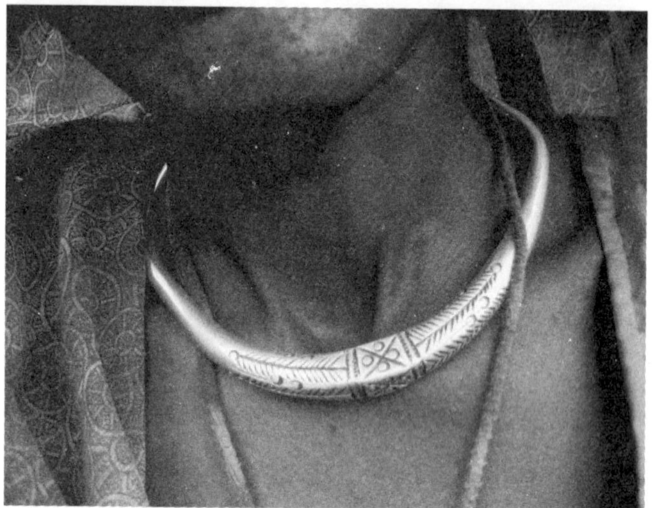

***Widow Marriage*:** Widow marriage is prevalent among Damors. Generally levirate marriage is popular. If the husbands younger brother refused to marry with his *Bhabhi* then the widow can marry with other person of her choice. In widow marriage *Dapa* is also taken by bride father. The widow marriage is arranged in a simple manner.

***Divorce*:** Divorce is permitted in this tribal group. Husband and wife both can seek divorce. Husband wishing to seek divorce is allowed but bound to compensate bride price to his wife. This *Jagda* is settled by the *Panch* of *Jati Panchayat*. If the divorce is sought by the wife no compensation is paid. In such a matter no *Jagda* is taken for divorce.

***Death Rituals*:** The dead body is cremated among Damors. The dead body of a child or that of a person died by smallpox is buried. Thirteen days of mourning is observed.

In the mourners house no food is cooked, the food and drinks are supplied by near kin to the family. The first ten days after death is observed as pollution period. On the 13th day the members of the tribe assemble at the residence of deceased person and turban tying ceremony is observed and a feast also given to guests. The eldest son of the deceased also gets turban called as *Sora Pagdi* from the villagers, which is sign of his recognition for succession. In Damors ashes are dispersed in holy rivers or nearby ponds according to their economic status.

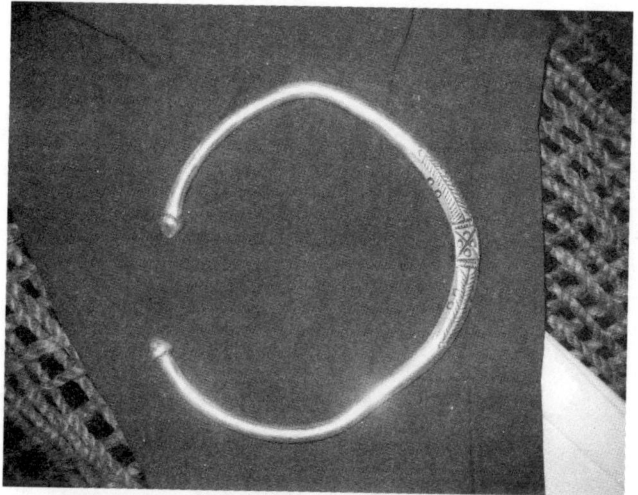

COSTUMES

Male Costumes

The male costumes of Damor tribe is exactly the same that of Bhil tribe. They wear *Dhoti, Kurta,* shirt and turban, *feta* or *feti.* The young generation have started to wear *pant,* shirt, T-shirt, *Nikker.*

Female Costumes

The female wear *ghaghra, petticoat, blouse* and *Odhni*. The petticoat is generally made by plain fabric, while *ghaghra* is printed one. The common prints in the *ghaghra* are floral prints. The length of *Odhni* is 1.5 metre and width is 1 metre only. The centre of the *Odhni* is tucked at head and both the ends are left open or sometimes tucked into the *ghaghra*. The bassom are not covered by the *odhni*. They remain bare. The girls also wear *petticoat, blouse, kurta* or shirt. They generally do not wear *odhni*. The school-going girls wear skirt and blouse, *salwar & kurta*. They generally prefer to wear red, yellow, orange, black, brown, grey, etc. coloured clothes.

Ornaments

Damor male also wear ornaments, but they are not fond of them. They generally wear chain in neck, *murki* or *ring* in ear and *kada* in wrist. Damor females are very much fond of ornaments. They generally wear *Bor* on head, *long* in nose, *capp, bali, tops* in ears, *chain, ahadi, hasli* and *mangalsutra* in neck, *bangdi* and *kada* in wrist, *vat;a* in finger, *toda* in ankle and *machali* in toe. Their ornaments are generally made by silver or any other cheap metal. *Long* of nose is generally made from silver or gold. They also wear bead ornaments like *mala, earnings,* etc.

Tattooing

Damor male only tattoo their name and any mark of diety on their hand or wrist. The Damor females are very much fond of tattoo. Every Damor female tattoo on her hand, head and along with feets. They generally tattoo their name on their hand with various designs viz. sun, star, flora, birds, etc.

CHAPTER 5

Garasia

Dr. Prakash Chandra Mehta

Garasia is the third largest tribal group of the state of Rajasthan. According to 1991 census 148,197 (75,899 males and 72,298 females) persons, constituting about 3 per cent of the total tribal population of the state. Though they are also found in the neighbouring state of Gujarat. Their main concentration is in the tehsils of Abu Road and Pindwara of Sirohi district, Bali in Pali district and Udaipur district; Kotra, Gogunda and Kherwara.

Origin

The word *Garasia* has its origin from Sanskrit word *Gras* meaning an orsel or subsistence. According to tradition, the Chauhan Rajputs of Jalore when defeated fled to the hills where subsequently they settled down on the grant of subsistence. They overpowered the Bhils, who were inhabitants of the region, and to pacify them also parted with some subsistence in their favour. There *Gras*-holders came to be known as the *Garasias.* They are only listed schedule tribe in the state of Rajasthan. The word *Garasia* is spelled differently viz. *Girasia, Grasia, Girrasia, Grasya* and *Girresseya.*

History

References of Garasia are found in the Medieval Rajput history. It is said that when the Rajputs were driven by the

Turks to this isolated region ruled by the Garasias, there emerged a confrontation between the two groups.

The tribal chiefs enjoyed their land by exploiting it and the Rajputs maintained their social status by making them headman of their areas with power to appoint village Patels.

The history records the help given by the Garasia to Maharana Udai Singh, Pratap, Amar Singh and other Rajput chiefs. The relations between Garasia and Maratha were not sweet. When the Maratha in 1731 entered the princely state of Dungarpur they also passed through *Bhomat* area. The Garasia has confrontation with the Maratha during the British period. All efforts were made to withdraw the concessions given to Garasias.

Inhabitation

The Garasia like scattered pattern of habitation villages. The Garasia term the *pal* as *patta*. There are two *pattas* among the Garasias of Sirohi belt: *Bhakar Patta* and *Pindwara Patta*. The *Bhakar Patta* consists of 24 villages which are clustered into three groups viz. Jambudi, Uplibore and Nichala Khejada. Every group have 8 villages, Jambudi is the oldest one, while other Pattas are (*Bhetar Patta)* 20 villages and *Pindwar Patta* (18 villages). Four *Pattas* in Udaipur district (1) Gogunda Patta-18 villages (2) Kherwara Patta-11 villages (3) Devla Patta-11 villages and (4) Pora Patta-5 villages, while in Gujarat state they are living in Palanpur Patta.

Like other tribal groups Garasia also lives in *kachha* houses made of mud and stones with thatched roof. These houses do not have any ventilation and sanitation facilities. Near the house they tie their animals in a courtyard. The fields of Garasias are located nearby their houses. The Garasia houses having fancing of local shurbs to protect their house.

Clan

The Garasia are territorially divided into two divisions viz. *Moti Jyat* (higher caste) and *Nanki Jyat* (lower caste). The division is basically spatial. The members of *Moti Jyat* consider themselves to be superior in terms of purity and pollution. They maintain higher code of conduct.

The Garasias having a number of clans and *atakhs*. Each traces its from a legendary father happened to be the founding ancestor. A clan is further sub-divided into *atakh* (Gotra). The clans form an exogamous group. The *astak* of the Garasia are named after plants, trees, vegetables, etc.

Family

The Garasia prefer a nuclear pattern of family in which parents and the unmarried sons and daughters lived together. After marriage, the son constructs a new house near the ancestorial enclosure. The father gave a piece of land to his son for his survival. After the death of the father property is equally divided among all sons. Generally, in

Garasias the youngest son, even after marriage, is required to stay with the parents.

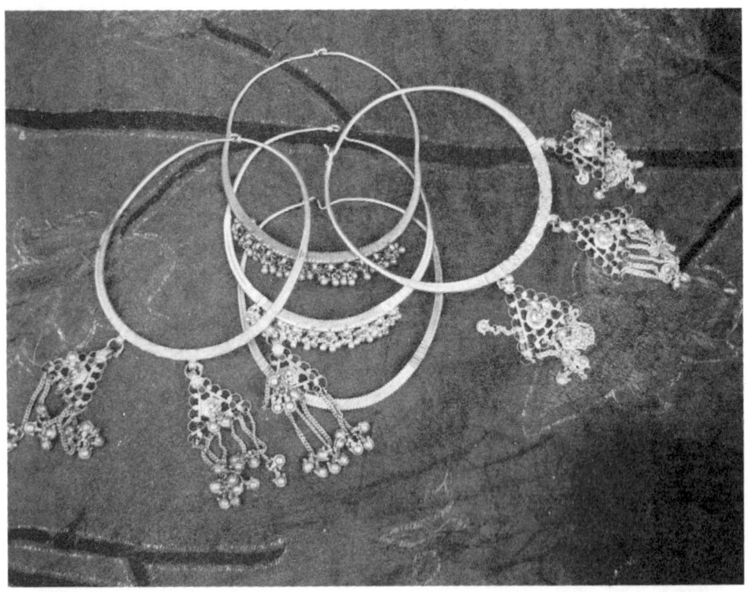

Life-cycle

Birth : Some women among the Garasias, on account of past traditions and empirical observations, are able to forefell the birth of a boy and girl after observing the movements of the pregnant mother. A Garasia father also observes some pre-natal and precautionary taboos. The family prepares for the arrival of the newcomer. The *Gotraj* is worshipped and indigenous medicines are kept ready. The birth of a girl is announced by beating winnowing fan (*Soopra*) and a boy by bronz plate (*thali*) by an elderly lady or mid-wife. The whole process of cutting and burying of *Vasuta* (placenta) called *amalamoriu*. On the seventh day after a delivery, the mother and child are taken to the *Vavsi* (local deity) with five small balls of *churma* and five handfulls of maize. Generally the mother is given two week rest, but few mothers attend to household jobs even after a week.

They observe Naming and *Mundan* ceremony. Naming ceremony is always arranged at holi when all the girls of the neighbouring houses are invited for selecting a good name for the newly born baby. Names are also given to signify days, months, *tithi,* place, flora and funa.

Marriage

Marriage among the Garasias is considered essential for both boy and girl. Among the Garasias the age of a man is calculated by his physical appearance, strength and capacity to earn.

Marriage by elopement is popular among Gasasias. They do not observe child marriage or infant betrothal. In Garasias a husband and wife can live together without performing a legal marriage, this is due to their poor economic condition because for marriage they are unable to arrange bride-price.

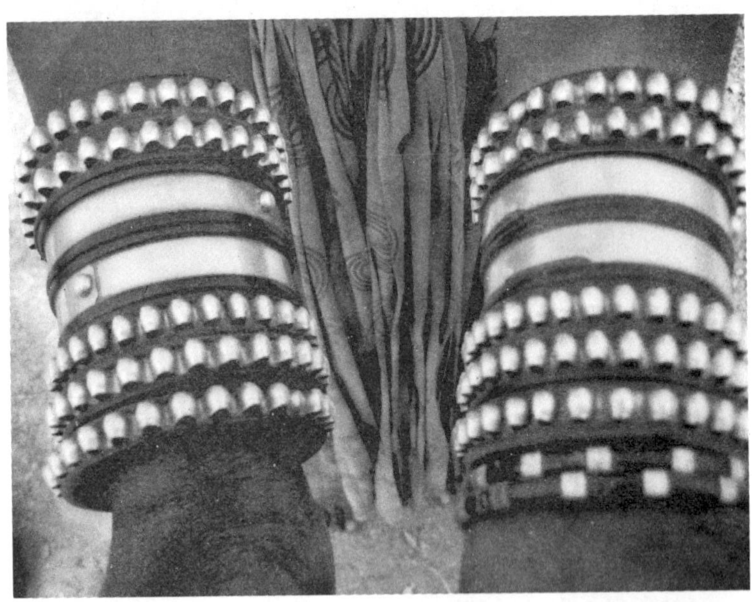

Monogamy is largely prevalent among Garasias. There are many types of marriages among the Garasias. The important types of marriages are: (1) *Morbandhiya* (2) *Melbo Marriage* (3) *Detwariya* (4) Service Marriage (5) *Ata-sasta* (Marriage by exchange) (5) Elopement and (7) *Natra*.

The main criteria of marriage is *dapa* (bride price). After fixing the bride price then *Sagai* is performed. If any dispute arises then *patels* or *Gameti* of both the villages settle this dispute. The most prevalent form of marriages in the Garasias are *Morbandhiya* and elopement. *Morbandhiya* marriage ceremony is performed with all the traditional ritual observed at boy and girl's houses. On this occasion they use ample liquor, give feast and sing songs by ladies. By this way they observe all the rituals from *sagai* to *vidai*. The important rituals are *Hangai, Gauri, Parla, Nutrate, Bethava, Pitti, Vandala, Manda, Jan hidi* and *Barr Kade*.

Widow marriage is permissible. Garasia women generally prefer to marry with her *devar*. If she wants to marry with other choice then bride-price is taken by her father. After fixing the bride-price (*data*), then she is allowed to marry with her choice. The widow marriage is performed in a simple manner.

Nata is also very common among Garasias. In case of *Nata* bride-price known as *Jaghra* is essential divorce can he seen in exceptional cases.

Death

To announce death a *Var* drum is beaten in a special way for three times and not more. During the funeral procession one the nearest male relative will carry fire and maize in earthen pots. In case of a death by smallpox and snake bite corpses are buried and not burnt. The *bhopas, devots* and *dakan* are not burnt but burried in the ground. There are many death ceremonies and rites observed by the Gasasias. Some of the important rites and ceremonies viz. *Hadk, Nyat, Phoolgholvu* and *Hurra.* Generally they observe thirteen days mourning. On thirteenth day they arrange a feast for nearest relatives and villagers.

COSTUMES

The costumes i.e. dress of Garasias are very attractive and colourful both in design and embroidery.

Male Costumes

Garasia male generally wear *dhoti, julki / bandi.* Now-a-days they also wear on the place of *julki / bandi, kurta* and shirt. The headgear of Garasia male consists of turban (*pagri*)-*potiyu,* the colour of which depends on the age and status–red colour for young and white for aged one. They also wear white *kurta, jhulki* with half sleeves shirt. They also use towel on the place of *potiyu* i.e. on the place of *pheta / pagri.* The *Patel,* the *Devata,* the *Bhopa* keep *pachroo* or *lattoo* on the shoulder when they go out. It is an indication of higher respectability in the society. Now-a-days the young Garasias also use to wear pant, shirt and T-shirt. The school-going children i.e. boys wear Pant, Shirt and Nikkar also. In social functions and dances. The Garasias till today wear their traditional costumes.

Female Costumes

The costumes of Garasia female are very colourful. Their costumes are very rich and few changes are reported. They are still following their traditional code of conduct in their dressing pattern.

Females are fond of all bright colours viz. yellow, orange, green, blue, red, etc. They do not have any restriction of colour. This tribal group is specially known for its colourful dressing.

The women generally wear *ghaghra, odhni* and *julki*. The *jhulki* is front open. It has two strings inside the side seams which is fastened first and then the two long strings which hang in the front of the *jhulki* is being tied. The strings are made-up of different colour fabric as that of *jhulki*. Multicolour small fabric triangles are added to the strive to make it attractive. The sleeve of the *jhulki* is full i.e. upto waist. The length of *jhulki* is upto mid of the thigh. It is stitched upto the waistline and below that four stripes falls. The edges of strips are decorated with the contrast fabric, embroidery and some multicolour triangle. Overall the *julki* make a Garasia women attractive. On the place of *julki* some women has started to wear blouse.

All the Garasia women, regardless of their age, they use to wear 8-20 metre width *Gherdar* printed or plain *ghaghra.* Contrast colour fabric is used for *Magji* at the hemline. This may be silver block printed or embroidered. The *ghaghra* is generally multicolour. Only widow or elderly Garasia women wear dark red or blue colour plain *ghedar ghaghra.* Now a days young female also wear pleated *ghaghra.* This type of *ghaghra* is prepared in 2.5 to 3 metre cloth with deep fold at the hemline. Side pleats are made in this *ghaghra.* The Garasia females do not prefer plain *ghaghra. Ghaghra* is generally decorated with *embroidery, silver block print* at the *magji,* mirror, *sitara* work, etc. They prefer only readymade and tailor-made garments.

Garasia women headdress is *odhni.* The *odhni* is square and made of 4 metre fabric i.e. length and width is 2 x 2 metre. The centre of *odhni* is draped on the head and both the ends fall on the sides of the hand. The bossom remain uncovered by the *odhni.* Generally they use plain *odhni* having golden lace on all the four sides. The floral print is most preferred for *odhni,* regarding the colour, all bright colours are used.

Ornaments

Garasia male are also found of ornaments. They only wear *murki* in ears, *kada* in wrist, *Mandlia* and *hankali* in the Neck and *kandora* in waist.

Garasia females are very fond of ornaments. They use to wear number of designer jewellery made of different materials. Their maximum jewellery is made through silver and some are of gold and beads. They wear *jhela* and *bor* on head, *long* in nose, *ognia, toti* and *barli*n in ears, *horki* (small), *horki* (Big), *hasli* and *haar* in neck, *chudi, boliyo, gajara* and *todiyan* in wrist *viti* and *hathful* in fingers, *kandora* in waist, *kada* and *pajab* in ankle and *bicchia* in Toe.

The weight of every ornament vary according to their preference. The females prefer heavy silver jewellery. The special jewellery of this tribal group is *haar* of mall bead of various colours. This type of *haar* is prepared by the *Garasia* women itself.

Tattooing

There is a practice of tattooing among the Garasia. Tattooing on face is called *Mandia* and on the body *Mandila.* Different flora and fauna, and animals viz peacock, scorpion, parrots, are designed on face and arms. Tattooing done with a mark of god or a deity might save the beholder from evil spirits. It is generally believed that tattooing brings happiness, love and pleasure in the life. Both male and female tattoo their name on their hands.

CHAPTER 6

Juang

Dr. Basanta Kumar Mohanta

The story of costume of a tribe or community presents a vital clue to their socio-economic conditions, their mood and taste, their aesthetic temper, their love for beauty and refinement, their art and skill to adjust to the material and geographical environment, their resourcefulness, their resilience to influences, external and internal, in short, their way of living. A historical pageant of costumes of a community or a nation is an essential aspect of its cultural heritage. No people can proud of without their heritage (Biswas 1985: 1). According to Ghurye (1995; Preface), "Costume, whatever might be its origins, provides the visible index of the homogeneity and the unity of a people or their absence". He further stated, the Indian males sport at least two more or less equally widely distributed and distinct varieties of dress. One variety, which may be described as the Northern and North-western consists of a long flowing coat, called '*jama*', for the upper part of the body and a kind of narrow trousers, called, '*pyjama*' or 'corana', for the lower part.... The other variety of the male costume may be called the Southern and North-eastern as it is principally met with in the North-eastern parts and in the regions south of the Narmada. It is based on '*dhoti*' as the lower garment and on a kind of tunic, called the '*kurta*' or a kind of long coat for covering the upper part of the body (Ghurye 1995: 14-15).

The Juang is a primitive tribe mainly depends upon the shifting cultivation and resides in a particular area of north-central Orissa. Until the middle part of the 20th century, they were wearing leaf dress and known as *Pattua* (the wearer of leaf dress). However, due to the interference of British and contact with the neighbouring communities they have gradually started using modern clothes of their neighbours. Although they have adopted the clothing of their neighbours, but had not left their traditional attire totally and continued it along with their new dress for a long period, as it was their tradition. Now-a-days this leaf-attire is a bygone tradition and is exists only in folklore and folk songs.

Since the pre-independent era, various scholars are working on the different aspects of the Juangs. In 1856, E. A. Samuells has for the first time written on the Juang tribe in the '*Journal of the Asiatic Society of Bengal*'. Following to him, Dalton (1872), Beglar (1882). Hunter (1877, 1893), O'Malley (1941), Risley (1891), Meik (1931), Elwin (1948) and Rout (1969-70) have made important works on the different aspects of the Juang tribe.

Besides, there are a number of scholars worked on the diverse field of the Juang tribe, such as, Behura (1992), Mohanti (1992) and Mohapatra (1989) worked on myth; Rout (1967-68) on folk songs; Das (1962), Prusty (1992) and Satpathy (1992) on the music, songs and dances; Rout (1967-68) and Das (1992) has studied the rituals and the religious belief; Dougal (1963, 1964) on social structure, categories and joking relations; Rout (1962, 1966-67) on Juang marriage. Similarly, Bose (1929) studied the clans and kinship, Dash (1989) worked on the kinship system, Rout (1963-64a, 1963-64b) and Kanungo (1992) on dormitory tradition, Mishra (1982) on folklore, Mohapatra and Mohapatra (1992) on language, Mohanty et al. (1992) and Sahoo, A.C. (1992) art, Rout (1966-67) and Sahoo, R. N. (1992) on Juang culture, Dash (1992) on ornaments; Patnaik (1986) on work, food intake, demography and fertility, Patnaik (1992) on work and population trend, Aparajita (1994) on integrated resources planning; Mohanty (1986) on shifting cultivation of the Juangs. Sahu (2007) has tried to describe the use and ownership of land whereas Srichandan (1992) has shown the impact of modernisation and industrialization of the Juang tribe at different time periods.

Area and the People

Orissa occupies a unique position in the tribal map of India. There are 62 tribal communities residing in the hinterland of Orissa of which 12 are identified as Primitive tribes. The Juangs–the shifting cultivator comes within this primitive tribal group. They are exclusively found in Orissa. They claims the Juang-Pirh of Keonjhar district as their homeland from where they have originated and gradually migrated to other parts of the Orissa. Presently these Juangs are mainly resided in the forested part of the Keonjhar district and its neighbouring area. The Juangs are broadly divided into two types, i.e. the *Hill Juang* and the *Plain Juang*. The *Hill Juangs* are inhabited in the hilly terrains and foothill of Keonjhar and Pallahara area and are still in a primitive stage. They mainly depended upon the shifting cultivation and minor forest produces. On the other hand, the Plain Juangs are mainly resided in the plains of Keonjhar and Angul (erstwhile in Dhenkanal district). They have adopted settled agriculture as their main occupation while a few have adopted basketry as their secondary occupation.

The word 'Juang' is a tribal dialect, which simply means as 'man', but the neighbours of the Juangs denote them as *'Pattua'* i.e. the wearer of leaf dress. The Juangs comes within the *Mundari* group. They possess medium stature and long head. The skin colour of the Juang varies from light brown to dark brown. They have their own dialects which itself known as Juang. With coming in contacts with their neighbouring people now they are also speaking Oriya. The Juangs reside in homogeneous village. The houses are scattered in the village. Although now it is not common but earlier, the *Hill Juangs* were frequently changing their village site and settlement. There were number of factors

Kattunaicken Woman in Natural Environment

Kattunaicken man

Mullukurumba Woman in Traditional Dress

Mullukurumba Man with Bow & Arrow

Juang Dancing Costume during 1970s (Courtesy : ROUT 1969)

Juang Girl in Traditional Leaf-Attire at Kantala, Pal Lahara State
(Courtesy : Elwin 1948)

An Old Woman of Barura Wore Sari and Beaded Ornaments
(Courtesy : ROUT 1969)

Adiyan—Moopan

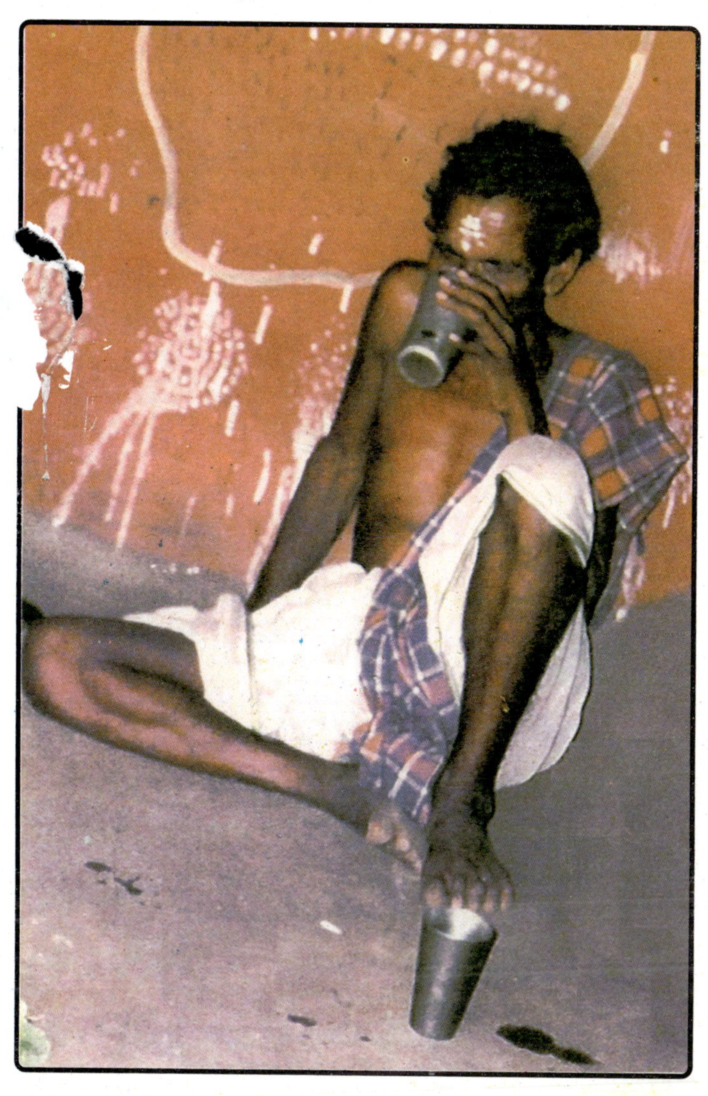

Present Costume of An Aged Male Member during Normal Time

Normal Dress of a Juang Youth at Work

Juang Woman Wearing Leaf-Attire As Drown by Strange
(J.A.S.B. Vol. XXV)

Normal Costume of a Juang Woman During 1970s
(Courtesy : ROUT 1969)

Usual Costume of a Juang Girl at Work

forced them to change their habitation sites. Some of the important factor includes, shortage or unfertile of the land for shifting cultivation, spread of epidemic and frequent death in the village etc. The *Majang* or *Mandaghar* is the youth dormitory of the Juangs, which is usually located at the center of the village. The Juangs are divided into a number of clans and each clan has their separate *totem*. They follow tribe endogamy and clan exogamy. The whole tribe is divided into two groups namely *Bandhu* clans and *Kutumb*. Monogamy is commonly practiced among the Juang but a few cases of polygamy is also found. Although the sororate and levirate is not found, but the divorce and remarriage is allowed.

The Juang believe in the supernatural power. The *'Dharm devta'* (sun god) is their supreme deity and the *'Basuki mata'* (earth goddess) is his counterpart. In every ritual, the Juangs worship them. The *'Rusi* and *'Rusiani'* are considered as their mythical ancestors and remembered in each occasion. The *Puspunei, Ambanua, Asadhi, Akshya Tritiya, Dhananua* etc. are their main festivals. The religious syncretism is clearly evident among the Juang. After coming in contact with their neighbouring wider pantheon they have also started worshipping different Hindu gods and Goddesses like, Laksmi, Mahadev, Parvati, Durga, Jagannath, Balabhadra, Rama and Sita, etc. The photographs of these deities are kept both in the houses and *majang* (youth dormitory) and worshipped at various occasions. The shifting cultivation is their main source of economy, but they are also depending upon the forest produces. Rice is their staple food which grown both in hills and plains.

The Juangs are very famous for their traditional dance and music. In spite of the poverty and food scarcity, they have retained their rich cultural heritage of colourful dance and music. Only through this cultural heritage, they express their inner feelings. The Juangs sing and dance when a group meets to another groups of opposite sex belonging to different clans. The *'changu'* dance of the Juang is very famous where the Juangs of both sexes dance together. Besides this *changu* dance, the Juangs also perform various kinds of dances such as, *elephant dance, bear dance, deer dance, pigeon dance, peacock dance*, etc. at different occasions.

COSTUMES

Till the mid of the 20th century the Juang were using their traditional leaf-attire. After coming in contact with their neighbouring communities and the then government agencies the Juang were forced to adopt the clothing of other communities which was a totally new to them. Although they were under pressure but since the beginning, this new clothing was not adopted totally by the Juangs. For a long period, they were using their traditional leaf-attire along with the adopted clothes in parallel way. Then slowly their traditional dress was disappeared from their life and culture and is replaced with the modern adopted dress. Based on the available data, the evolution of the Juang costume can be broadly divided in to three phases, i.e. (a) Phase-1 (before 1948), (b) Phase-ll (in between 1948 and 1970) and (c) Phase-III (after 1970). During the first half of the 20th century, Col. Dalton, V. Elwin etc. had made a very thorough study to this primitive tribe, which is basically analysed in Phase-I of the article. After the Independence of India, the government has given special emphasis for the development of these tribal. During this time, both the government agencies as well as scholars of the relevant field started documenting the various aspects of the Juangs. The new costume of the Juangs, which was documented in between 1948 and 1970, are mainly analysed in Phase-II of this article. Many developmental works have been made in the Juang area by both the government and non-government agencies. Now-a-days the government is giving special attention to provide all kinds of essential needs to the Juangs. All the villages are connected with the main roads. Because of this communication and transportation facilities the people of the outer world are easily accessing in to the Juang land

and vice-versa. The present (after 1970) costume of the Juangs is described in phase-III, which is continuing till date with minor addition.

Phase-I (Before 1948) : During the beginning stage of the second half of 19th century, E. A. Samuells has for the first published on the Juang tribe in the *'Journal of the Asiatic Society of Bengal* where he mentioned, "The dress of the men is ordinary one of the native peasantry, but the women wear no clothes whatsoever. Their only covering consists of two large branches of leaves (or rather of twigs with the leaves attached). It is from this original custom that the tribe have obtained from their neighbours the name of *Puttoos quasi the people of the leaf*....No covering is worn on the upper part of the person; but most of the females I have seen had necklaces of coloured earthernware beads (made by themselves they told me)" (Samuells 1856).

Following to it, Col. Dalton has described about the leaf dress of the Juangs women. In *'Descriptive Ethnology of Bengal* where he wrote, "in habits and customs the most primitive people" he had "met with or read of, and he considered the Juang as survival "of the stone age *in situ"* (Dalton 1872). Analyzing the view of Dalton, Elwin (1948: 39) mentioned, "had not amongst them a particle of clothing, their sole covering for purposes of decency consisted in a girdle composed of small curtains of leaves. Adam and Eve sewed fig leaves together and made themselves aprons. The Juangs are not so far advanced; they take young shoots of the *Asan (Terminalia tomenlosa)* or any tree with long soft leaves, and arranging them to form a flat and scale-like surface of the required size, the springs are simply stuck in the girdle fore and aft and the toilet is complete. The girls were well developed and finely formed specimens of the race, and as the light leafy costume left the outlines of the figure entirely nude, they would have made good studies for a sculptor".

The Juangs are a danceous and gay people. Earlier the changing of a leaf dress in each day was essentially for a

Juang woman before going dance. Without changing their dress, they were feeling uncomfortable. According to Dalton (Dalton 1872: 155), whilst he was conversed with the males on their customs, language and religion, the girls sat nestled together in a corner, for a long time silent and motionless as statues, but after an hour or two had elapsed the crouching nymphs showed signs of life and symptoms of uneasiness, and more attentive regarding them. He noticed great tears were dropping from the downcast eyes like dew drops on the green leaves. When he wanted to know the reason behind it he was told, the leaves were becoming dry, stiff, and uncomfortable, and if they will not permit to go to *jungle* for replacing these leave, the result would be not good, and they will be not able to take part in dance. In *A Statistical Account of Bengal,* W. W. Hunter (1877) has mentioned about the traditional dress of the Juangs as, "The men wore a single cotton cloth. The women had not even this, but simply a string round their waist, with a bunch of leaves before and behind". In his book *The People of the Leaves* Vivian Meik (1931) has presented a picture of the Juang, which is far away from the truth and reality. There are various kinds of folklore and legends available relating to this leaf-dress of the Juang. Some time these legends are contradictory to each other. In one hand some stories narrated about the evolution of their dress pattern that how initially they were naked adopted leaf-attire and on the other hand some stories argued the Juang as dressed and even well-dressed in silk or cotton cloth and their leaf attire due to a curse laid upon them.

As mentioned, the Juangs were wearing leaf-attire. Elwin (1948: 40) had collected a folklore related to this leaf-dress from *Pallahara*. The folklore is as follows. Once upon a time, there was a "Rusi and his wife lived on roots. When they had many children Rusi said to his wife, 'Formerly we were but two and we did well on roots. But what are we to do with the children?' His wife said, 'Feed them on roots like ourselves. So, they went to dig for roots for their children. When they found the place the woman sat down to dig and

Rusi stood by. She spread out her legs and her thing visible. Rusi saw it and turned his head away. His wife said, 'What are you looking at? Why don't you look at me?' but he looked away all the more. The wife went on talking but he said not a word. Then she wearied and cried. 'O Mahapurub! Why won't he talk to me?' Mahapurub came to her and said, 'Go to the kumi tree and pick its leaves for a dress.' But she did not know how to put on the leaves. Mahapurub himself picked fourteen leaves and tied seven in front and seven behind. When he saw that Rusi cried, 'She is Patharsarni indeed, and began to laugh loudly.' He himself made a belt of the kumi bark and wore it.

Here modesty seems to be the motive for dressing. In a Keonjhar legend it is vaguely connected with the beginning of menstruation.

In the old days, all men lived naked. They did not even wear leaves. Men and women lay down together naked on the ground. One day a house-rat bit a woman between her thighs and blood flowed from the place. Rusi saw it and made women wear leaves. Because the rat put its nose into the vagina, if ever it touches water the water stinks.

Some of the folk stories are associated to the leaf-attire and the Hindu mythology of Mahabharata period. Elwin had collected a folk story from Phanasnasa, which relates the leaf-attire with Bhima and the discovery of fire. The story is as follows, "Their lived an Asur. It was devouring men. Of the five Pandava brothers all were married but the youngest Bhima. He built a Darbar for himself and lived there. He taught the people to eat roots. There was no fire in those days. The five brothers went to hunt and night fell. They sent Bhima to look for fire. In the jungle was the daughter of that Asur. Bhima came to her house and asked for fire. She said, 'Here I sit naked in my house; how can I come out to give you fire?' Bhima made a dress of leaves and threw it in to her. She put it on and gave him fire.

When Bhima rejoined his brothers with the fire, they said, 'You are very late; why have been so long? When he told them what had happened, they said, 'You have given her a dress and you have made her your's. You must marry her.' The girl's name was Patrosurni. The Asur fought against him, but Bhima destroyed him. He married the girl and they lived together in the jungle. Thus the Juang began and wore leaves. It was because Bhima ate roots and lived in the Darbar that he was strong enough to defeat the Asur" (Elwin 1948: 40-42).

At the initial stage the Juangs were remain naked and gradually adopted leaf-attire to part or whole of their body which is clear from these two above mentioned stories. But there are some contradictory folklore also available which are totally different from these folk stories relating to this evolution of cloth. Example may be cited from two folk stories collected by Elwin in 1948 from Kantala and Gonasika. The first story is as follows, "We are Rusi-putro, the sons of Naiko Rusi. When we were born he gave us beautiful clothes, long strips of silk for dhoti, sari or turban. But one day during the Pus Punni Festival the women finished all the work of the house except the cow-dunging. They went to bathe and returned with wet clothes. They thought, 'If we cow-dung the floors now, our clothes will be spoilt.' They took their clothes off, dressed themselves in leaves and so cow-dunged the floors. At this time Dharam Deota came by and seeing them was angry. 'I gave you fine clothes, and you've gone and dressed yourselves in leaves. Very well, from today you will be Pathar-paharoni Juang, leaf-wearing Juang.' So saying he took away their clothes and disappeared." (Elwin 1948: 42).

The second story is also the same like the previous one. "According to this the sons and daughters of Rusi went to dance at Gonasika and when they got home they found their houses filthy. They began to cow-dung the floors and soon dirtied the beautiful clothes that Dharam Deota had given to them. They looked at their bottoms and could see nothing but cow-dung. So they took off their clothes, put on leaves and went on with their work. Dharma Deota said, 'I have given you good food and good clothes, yet you wear leaves.' 'But we are doing to save our clothes.' 'If you want to save them, you will lose them.' He sent them to wear leaves and eat fruit and roots in the jungle" (Elwin 1948: 42).

The Baitarani is considered as one of the most sacred river of India. It takes its origin from Gonasika and passes through the different parts of the northern Orissa. This Gonasika is also considered as the center place of the Juang-Pirh from where the Juangs have originated and migrated to other areas. There are some folk stories, which link this sacred river and the leaf-attire of the Juang. According to Dalton (1872: 156) this tradition of leaf-attire of the Juang is a Brahmanical origin. Supporting his statement he has mentioned, There are several; the simplest and prettiest is connected with the origin of the Baitarani. The river goddess emerging for the first time from the Gonasika rock, came suddenly on a rollicking party of Juangs dancing naked, and ordering them to adopt leaves at that moment as a covering, laid on them the curse that they must adhere to that costume for ever or die'. Continuing this story Dalton is told '....for the Juangs rather than by them. Their own idea simply is the converse of the rule of civilized nations. They deem that the fashion of dress should never change, and that for females especially it should be simple and cheap'. He further mentioned, 'The notion must tend to conserve the Juangs in their present habits of hill and forest life. They must be where there is a plentiful supply of the material of nature's providing. It have not heard of any of the tribe having settled in places where it would be difficult to follow their inclination in dress.' (Dalton 1872: 156).

Besides, there are some other stories, which also describe and link the leaf-attire of the Juang along with the Hindu mythology. One of such type of story is presented here. Once Markand Rusi tore his loincloth into four pieces. He kept one piece with him and gave two to his two sons and one to his two daughters. As two daughters gets only one piece of cloth it was not possible for them to wear it by both of them at a same time. Therefore, one wore it and the other wore leaves. One daughter who wore that small piece of cloth becomes a Bhuiyan and who wore leaves becomes a Juang.

To discuss about the method of collection of this leaf-attire, their disposal and associated superstition, Elwin had mentioned, "The leaf-dress is a simple and natural one. So long as the Juang live to themselves in the recesses of their hills, so long as there are no outside eyes to pry and stare, it is well adapted to the innocent ways of the people. Any kind of large leaf can be used. The leaves are brought from the jungle in the early morning, laid on the ground in rows and pressed flat with earth or stones. A girdle is made with a large number of bugles of baked earth which are threaded onto strips of bark-cord; the girdle is a substantial thing; fairly heavy, sometimes as thick as a dozen or fifteen rows of cords and bugles. The leaves are stuck into this by the springs so as to form thick aprons back and front; the loins are left uncovered.

These leaves are full of magic, and have to be carefully protected. The previous day's leaves are thrown away very early in the morning while it is still dark, not even the husband knowing where. They are thrown into a pit and the wearer spits on them. Great care must be taken to pick up any leaf or bit of leaf that fals from the girdle. Once, when *Sat* was in the world, wherever one of the leaves fell a spring of water appeared. But now that there is no more *Sat* in the jungle tribe, if a leaf is left on the ground and someone treads on it, the wearer may die. If the parents of a girl trod on the leaf or stepped over it, it would be a sin equivalent to incest. If a witch could get hold of the leaf, she could send a tiger to devour the wearer or snake to bite her; she could make her barren or unclean. 'One day a sahib came from Cuttack and there was a dance in Pal Laharagarh. When some of the leaves fell to the ground, the people were afraid to pick them up. Two or three days later a girl was eaten by a tiger at Kantara. Since then we have always picked up the leaves very carefully.' And indeed it is an amusing sight to watch the group of old women with long sticks hovering round a Juang dance watching for any scrap of leaf that may fall down. Immediately there is a rush for it, it is picked up and carefully preserved and buried' (Elwin 1948: 43).

The Juangs were very simple and they had a very close relationship with their surrounding nature. They were not interested to discontinue their age old tradition of leaf-attire. According to Elwin (1948: 43), after the hundred years of introduction of modern civilization it has given nothing to the Juangs. They do not have any kind of health and education facilities not got any training in agriculture and industry. However, the people of the outer world were forcing them to leave the leaf-attire. Citing a semi-official account of what was done, by L.S.S. O'Malley (1941: 733), who bases his facts on a passage in Hunter's *The Indian Empire* (1893). He has mentioned, in 1871 an attempt was made by the British government to introduce the civilized cloth among the Juangs. They tried to replace it in place of their traditional leaf-attire. Those Juangs who came within the sphere of British influence were forced to wear these cloths by order of the then government, and their chief was persuaded to do the same good work for others. Apart from this, an English officer called a meeting of the tribe where he distributed about 2000 clothes to the women. After his return, they gathered all the clothes in a heap and burnt (O'Malley 1941: 733). According to Risley (1891: 352) the officer responsible for this vandalism was Captain F.J. Johnstone, Superintendent of the Keonjhar state, 'who had acquired great influence with the people. In 1874 J.D. Beglar of the Archaeological Survey visited Baitarani who noticed the leaf-attire has been changed, but according to him, 'It struck me as somewhat incongruous that the men were dressed much more decently then the woman, and reason assigned was that women are so seldom out in places of public resort that they do not need it.' *(Archaeological Survey Reports* 1882 XIII: 771).

The Juangs have some superstition about the forcefully leaving of their traditional attires. The uselessness of introducing the outer garb of civilization without doing anything to promulgate its spirit is seen in the effect, which this action had upon the Juang. This forcefully leaving of their traditional dress gave a great psychological and spiritual shock to the Juangs from where they could not able to recover themselves. They remember that day when their sacred leaves were burnt as a conquered nation recalls the day of its defeat. The Juangs believe that from that day, the *Sat* (the spirit of the truth and religion, the power to live safely in a world of hostile magic) has left them. In a result, the tigers attacked their cattle and the offended earth gives but a very little crop. Citing some typical examples of this superstition of the Juangs, Elwin (1948: 44-45) has given some examples, which are presented below.

"In Gonasika the Juang Naiko said, 'In Godadaro Raja's time a sahib came here and gave us cloth and made us burn our leaves. Since that day truth and religion has left us. Whatever we may sow we get poor crops. Every kind of wild animal attacks us. Before then Thakurani Mahapat (the earth mother) was pleased with us and whenever we spoke to her she answered. But those days are gone."

In Phanasnasa, the Juang said, Jinkini Sahib came to Gonasika and called us to dance before him. He stood up and said, "You wear leaves. That is shameful. It is the order of Government that you should stop. I will give you cloth instead." Our Dihuri replied, "The leaves were given us by Dharam Deota. If we wear cloth we will die or tigers will eat us." The sahib gave two cows, two sheep and two goats to please the gods. Then he took away the leaves and gave cloth instead, and forced the Dihuri to burn the leaves with his own hands.'

An another account from Balipal: 'Jinkini Sahib brought many boxes of cloth to Gonasika. He called the Juang and said to them, "Do you know what is in these boxes?" They answered, "Kal (danger)." He laughed and opened the boxes and inside there was nothing but snakes. The sahib said, "But I filled these boxes with cloth. How are they full of snakes"? Our Dihuri said, "If you say it is cloth it will be"– and immediately everybody saw that it was cloth. The sahib began to distribute the cloth. An old woman went into the jungle to put it on and was at once eaten by a tiger. So we offered many sacrifices to stop the tigers, bears and snakes and then put on the cloth. The women wept loudly, for they hated the cloth and we too wept for we saw the ruin of our race. Since that time wild elephants have begun to destroy our fields and kill us" (Elwin 1948: 44-45).

Although the Juangs had adopted clothes by coming in contact with different people and forces but the Juang women were putting a few pieces of leaves inside their clothes to continue their tradition and to protect themselves from the magico-religious practices. Narrating the continuation of this tradition of the Juang, Elwin (1948: 45-46) has mentioned, "Nothing reveals Juang feeling more clearly than the fact that the now vague and shadowy figure of '*Jinkini*' has been partly identified with the abominable Pig King who, as he lay dying, anticipated *Jinkini's* commands and threatened his subjects with death if they wore their leaves.

In Keonjhar and Dhenkanal the leaf-dress soon became a thing of the past. But it survived in Pal Lahara. N.K. Bose found women wearing leaves in 1928 and I did so also in 1942 and everywhere there are certain survivals. Many Juang women wear a few leaves under their cloth as a magical protection. At a wedding the bride is attired in her traditional leaf-dress. At dances the Juang put on their leaves with the utmost willingness and are evidently delighted to have any excuse to do so. The belief in the power of the worn leaf is as strong as ever. When a witch goes out on her dark business, she puts on leaves. She kills her man goes at night to a cross-road, dresses in leaves and worships.

In place of the clean and lovely leaves, that look so beautiful in their bright greenery against the golden brown of the skin, the Juang women now wear filthy little scraps of cloth that are less decent than the ample leaves, less artistic, and infinitely less hygienic.

Phase-II (In between 1948 and 1970): By the time, the Juangs have already adopted and assimilated the costume of their neighbouring communities. Although the Juang have adopted the *dhoti* and *sari* as their dress, but they do not have sufficient clothing to use. Therefore, they were using a single piece of cloth for a long period. They specially decorate themselves for dance. Describing about the dress of the Juang during the middle part of the 20th century, Rout (1969-70: 17) has mentioned. The women not having sufficient clothings so they cannot wash their clothes daily. The men take nacked bath in streams. Clothes are washed with soaps purchased from market or by boiling them with ashes. The plains Juang are not doubt more particular in washing their clothes than the hill Juang who never mind it much.

Comparing the dress of the Juang with their neighbouring tribe Bhuinya Rout (1969-70: 17) has stated, "In dressing their head the Juang are not so particular like the Bhuinya. They comb their hair by bamboo combs made by themselves in Keonjhar, and by wooden combs purchased from market in Dhenkanal. On the hills, the men have long hair to grow to a certain length; but on the plains this fashion is out of date and is looked down upon by others. The men comb their head daily after bath, but the women comb their hair once or twice a month. The girls do it more frequently on the day of going to the market, to the fair, or while going to their *bandhu* villages on dancing expeditions. The girls make a long and cylindrical bun adding a bunch of red and yellow ribbons, and decorate their bun with a brass hair-pin. They use *kusum* oil (*bangrur aian*), *rasi* oil (*ramtilaaian*), or mustard oil. Coconut oil is too dear for them to use."

Phase-III (After 1970): Now-a-days the Juangs wear the common dress as worn by the other neighbouring people of the region. The women wear *sari* and the man put on *dhoti.* The children usually wear napkins whereas the school going children use shirt and pants. The women decorate themselves with various types of ornaments like bangles, nose rings, earrings, anklets, armlets, etc. These ornaments are made of brass or alloy. They also use necklaces of various designs made of coloured beads. Tattooing on the forehead and arms are usually noticed among the women, which is very common to decorate their body.

Normally, the Juangs wear scanty dresses. The present costume of the Juang is almost same like their neighbouring communities. A single piece of unsewn cloth i.e. a *dhoti* and a *sari* is the basic garment for a man and a women respectively. *Dhoti* has frontal pleats and a posterior tuck. A portion of *sari* is worn like a skirt with frontal pleats and the remaining portion is used for covering the upper part of the body. *Dhoti* may accompany an upper garment like *chadar, ganji* or shirt or may remain a lone garment. *Sari* is worn over a *saya* (petticoat) and blouse. *Sari* is also worn without any accompaniments in some Juangs women. These *sari* and *dhoti are* said to be the modern version of the clothes the Juang used to wear, though the woman's garment is now used to cover both the lower and the upper parts of the body. The details of their dressing pattern is given below.

Male Costume

The aged male members like to wear a short *dhoti* of about three to four metre long, or any shorter garment usually girded above the knees. These *dhotis* are either handloom or mill-made and mainly white in colour. They occasionally wear shirt during their festivals or on journeys out of the village or local market centers. Because of this, the upper part of the body of most of the aged Juang is usually left bare. Sometimes a short piece of cloth *(gamchha* or *taulia)* is wound round the head. The usual lower garment of a middle aged men folk is either a *dhoti, lungi* or a shorter garment which hardly extends upto the knees, a small piece of cloth *(gamchha* or *taulia)* folded lengthwise and is either tied round the loins or slung on the shoulder. During their agricultural and other activities, sometime it is also tied round the head to protect it from hot or dust. The boys usually prefer to wear readymade half-pants. It covers hardly until their knees. The minor children remain naked. The school-going boys use shirt. However, after returning from school, the wearing up of shirt and *banyan* is not compulsory. Sometime they wear only *banyan* or left the upper half of the body bare. They also like to hang a lengthwise folded *gamchha* on their shoulder or round the loins. The small children rarely, on specific occasion like festival or any socio-cultural gatherings, wear shirts and pants. The Juang do not prepare these dresses. They purchase these clothes from nearby market centers and weekly markets.

Female Costumes

The women wear *sari* with a very thin border. Its free end is thrown back over the left shoulder and then brought back to be tucked in on the left waist. The length of the cloth reaches down up to the calves. While at work the end of the *sari* is rolled round along the waist, but otherwise the upper edge is so neatly tucked that the end is displayed with its full width on the front. The Juang women prefer the deep coloured printed *sari*. The use of petticoat along with *sari* is found among the middle aged Juang women. Although the Juang women like to use thick and deep coloured petticoat, these are plane and not printed. The aged Juang woman do not use blouse. The coarse *saris* are used to cover both of the upper and lower part of their body. However, the middle-aged women prefer to use the blouse along with the *sari*. During the normal time, the petticoat and *sari* cover until the feet. But at the time of their agricultural activities, domestic work like besmearing of cow dung solution on the floor, moving around the forest, they like to fold the petticoat along with the lower portion of the sari till the knee portion. Use of inner bodice is recently introduced among the younger generation of the female folk. They worn blouse on this inner bodice, which covers their shoulder and breast portion. The center of upper portion of the blouse is cut either rounded or slightly pointed as low as propriety would permit. The lower portion of the blouse is extended so that it could be tucked inside the *sari* or displayed over it as a stomacher. They do not use any type of under-garments whatsoever. The infant children generally move naked. The grown up children try to cover their genital organs by a small piece of cloth. An additional *chaddar* or cotton cloth is used in winter season to protect them from chill winter.

Ornaments

The female members decorate themselves with various kinds of ornaments. Earlier the Juangs were using girdle made of small tubes or beads or burnt clay. They were also decorating themselves with necklaces of glass beads, and brass ornaments in their ears and on their wrists (Elwin 1948: 39). But, now-a-days they prefer bangles, anklets, nose rings, toes rings, earrings, armlets made of brass or alloy. They also like to use the beaded necklace of various design and colours. According to Dash (1992: 50-51), the "Juangs are a danceous and gay people and the rings decorate their fingers on the leg and hands. Similarly, the anklets are the musical sound generating ornaments used during dancing performances. As these ornaments decorate, their person is made or designed to stick to the woman and may not get loose and slip away at the time of dance. Hence, the rings and anklets are small and remain tight on the body of the dancers as appears from the objects". At the time of describing about the Juang costume at the time of their dance, Das (1962: 128) has mentioned that in the earlier days the Juang women were putting on the leaf dresses to cover the lower half of their body. The upper half of the body was bedecked with a few necklaces. They also used this similar type of dress at the time of dance. However, with the change of time the girls started wearing *sari*. The common types of ornaments used by the female dancers are *noli* (earring), *katadi, bainsi* (bracelets), *anklets, chaunrimundi* (head ornament) and brass rings. The male dancers usually wear *dhoti* and turbans made by napkins.

The Juangs use various kinds of rings and anklets. Based on the number of circle wires attached at the top with some patterns. These rings are purposefully designed in order to make easy during dancing. The anklets used by the Juangs dancers contian another aspects of their art depiction. The design of these anklets can be divided into two types. The first type of anklets contains a hollow tubular round shaped form with plain ends facing each other. The upper surface is provided with interlocking hooks to make room for the attachment of bolls. Although the second type of anklet is also contains the hollowed tubular form, but it possesses a denticulate jafri-patterned decoration in both of the faces with ring-type attachments on the upper rim surface meant for the bells.

Tattooing

The body decoration of the female shows the artistic talent of the Juang. The females are very much fond of tattooing. The tattooing on the arms and forehead is evident among the females. As mentioned earlier the *Dharam devta* or sun god is considered as the supreme deity of the Juang. They believe that if some impression of this great god remains in the body, there will be no danger. Therefore, the Juang women like to keep this sun motif on their body. They know that this tattoo is the only thing what they will carry with them after their death. Apart from this, the Juang women also like to paint their hands, legs, and chests with different types of geometric designs. These tattoo are made on the body with a very crude process. At the time of tattooing, they apply a special kind of black on that pinching portion, which never fade from their body and last long.

Man is a cultural animal and each stage of cultural evolution brings change in human life and culture. It may in their food habit, economy, folklore, folksongs, religious life and in the costumes also. When a new trait of culture comes into the life and culture of a tribe or community first of all the people of that particular tribe or community tested its advantages and then adopt it partially or fully as per their requirement, which gradually assimilated and became a part of their culture. The similar thing is happened in case of the Juang costumes. Traditionally the Juangs were using the leaf-attire, which continued until the early part of the 20th century. This traditional dress was very much attached to their religious life, folklore and mythology. However, soon after the interference of the British administration and contact with their neighbourers they slowly started replacing their traditional attire into cloth. However, as this leaf-attire was very much attached to their religious life it was not very easy for them to leave it totally. Therefore, although the Juang women had started wearing *sari* but they put few pieces of leaf inside their cloth not only to continue their tradition but also to protect themselves from the evil spirits and black magic. They were keeping these leaves specially when they were going to attend a social gathering or to participate in a ritual. However, now-a-days this tradition of leaf-attire has been totally changed and the Juangs are using clothes like their neighbouring communities on all occasions.

REFERENCES

1. Aparajita, Upali (1994): Multi-Level Analysis for Integrated Resources Planning: A Case Study of the Juangs. *The Journal of the Anthropological Survey of India.* 43 (3 & 4): 87-100.
2. Beglar, J.D. (1882): *Archaeological Survey Reports,* Vol. XIII. Calcutta.
3. Behura, N.K. (1992): "Myth as the Ideological Order Among the Juangs". In Dash, R.N. edited *Art and Culture of the Juang.* Bhubanesar; Orissa Lalit Kala Akademi, pp. 19-25.

4. Biswas, A. (1985): *Indian Costumes.* New Delhi; Publication Division, Ministry of Information and Broadcasting.
5. Bose, N. K. (1929): Juang Associations. *Man in India* IX: 19-29.
6. Dalton, E.T. (1872): *Descriptive Ethnology of Bengal.* Calcutta.
7. Das, H.C. (1992): "Songs and Dance of the Juangs of Dhenkanal", *Orissa Historical Research Journal* XI (2).
8. Das, H.C. (1992): "Religious Beliefs and Practices of the Juangs". In Dash, R. N. edited *Art and Culture of the Juang.* Bhubanesar; Orissa Lalit Kala Akademi, pp. 61-68.
9. Dash, J. (1989): "Juang kinship terms: An Analysis". *Adibasi* XXIX (No. 324): 29-38.
10. Dash, R. N. (1992): "Juang Art in Rings and Anklets". In Dash, R. N. edited *Art and Culture of the Juang.* Bhubanesar; Orissa Lalit Kala Akademi, pp. 50-61.
11. Elwin, V. (1948): "Notes on the Juang". *Man in India* 28 (1 & 2): 1-116.
12. Ghurye, G.S. (1995): (First published in 1951): *Indian Costume.* Bombay; Popular Prakashan.
13. Hunter, W.W. (1877): *A Statistical Account of Bengal.* London. Vol. XIX.
14. Hunter, W.W. (1893): *The Indian Empire.* London, p. 94.
15. Kanungo, J.C. (1992): "Dormitary Tradition of the Juang". In Dash, R. N. edited *Art and Culture of the Juang.* Bhubanesar; Orissa Lalit Kala Akademi, pp. 85-89.
16. Mc. Dougal, C. (1963): "The Social Structure of the Hill Juang"–A Precis". *Man in India* 43 **(3)**
17. Me. Dougal, C. (1964): "Juang Categories & Jocking Relations." *South-Western Journal of Anthropology* 20 (4).
18. Meik, Vivian (1931): The *People of the Leaves.*
19. Mishra, K.C. (1982): "Aspects of Juang Folklore." *Adibasi* XXI (1-4): 11-38.
20. Mohanti, K. K. (1992): "The Juang Origin Myth." *Adibasi* XXXII (4): 1-8.
21. Mohanty, B. (1986): "Shifting Cultivation in Orissa: with a case study among the Juang." *Adibasi* XXVI (3):17-26.
22. Mohanty, K. K., B. Chowdhury and A. C. Sahoo (1992): "The Juang Artistic Experience". In Dash, R. N. edited *Art and Culture of the Juang.* Bhubanesar; Orissa Lalit Kala Akademi, pp. 1-6.

23. Mohapatra, K. and Sasmita Mohapatra (l992): "Juang Gata." In Dash, R. N. edited *Art and Culture of the Juang.* Bhubanesar; Orissa Lalit Kala Akademi, pp. 26-32.

24. Mohapatra, P.K. (1989): "Myths of Juang–An Anthropological Analysis". *Adibasi* XXIX (No-324): 21-23.

25. O'Malley, L.S.S. (1941): *Modern India and the West.* London. p. 733.

26. Patnaik, N. (1986): "The Juangs of Orissa: their work and food intake, demography and fertility." *Adibasi* XXVI (3): 25-65.

27. Prusty, R. P. (1992): "The Juang Dance." In Dash, R. N. edited *Art and Culture of the Juang.* Bhubanesar; Orissa Lalit Kala Akademi, pp. 78-84.

28. Risley, H.H. (1891): *Tribes and Castes of Bengal.* Vol. 1, p. 352. Calcutta.

29. Rout, S.P. (1962): "Types of Marriages among the Juang of Keonjhar District, Orissa." *The Orissa Historical Research Journal* XI (3).

30. Rout, S. P. (1963-64a): "Dormitory Organisation of the Juang of Keonjhar." *Adibasi* **1.**

31. Rout, S. P. (1963-64b): "Functions of Juang Dormitory in Keonjhar District." *Adibasi* **2.**

32. Rout, S. P. (1966-67): "Economic Aspects of Juang Marriage." *Adibasi* **3.**

33. Rout, S. P. (1966-67): "The Juang and Culture Change." *Adibasi* **1.**

34. Rout, S. P. (1967-68): "Socio-Economic Implications of Pus Punei Ritual of the Hill Juang of Keonjhar." *Adibasi* IX (2).

35. Rout, S. P. (1969-70): Handbook of the Juang. *Adibasi* XI (1 & 2):1-16.

36. Sahoo, A. C. (1992): "The Juang Art–A Socio- Cultural Perspective." In Dash, R. N. edited *Art and Culture of the Juang.* Bhubanesar; Orissa Lalit Kala Akademi, pp. 7-18.

37. Sahoo. R. N. (1992): "Culture of the Juang at a Glance." In Dash, R. N. edited *Art and Culture of the Juang.* Bhubanesar; Orissa Lalit Kala Akademi, pp. 90-92.

38. Sahu, Champak (2007): "*Use and Ownership of Land of the Juang in Keonjhar.*" Unpublished Ph.D. thesis submitted to Utkal University.

39. Samuells, E.A. (1856): *Journal of the Asiatic Society of Bengal.* XXV.

40. Satpathy, S.K. (1992): "Juang Music and Dance." In Dash, R. N. edited *Art and Culture of the Juang,* Bhubanesar; Orissa Lalit Kala Akademi, pp. 69-77.

41. Srichandan, G.K. (1992): "Modernisation-cum-Industrialisation of Tribal Societies in Orissa." In Dash, R.N. edited *Art and Culture of the Juang.* Bhubanesar; Orissa Laiit Kala Akademi, pp. 42-49.

CHAPTER 7

Kathodi

Dr. Prakash Chandra Mehta

The Kathodi alias Katkari meaning catechu makers is an isolated primitive community in Rajasthan. They are the migrants from Songarh and Nawapur in Maharashtra. Both the names of the tribe, Kathodi meaning *Katha* or Catechu makers and Katkari meaning a wood cutter or a person engaged in occupations like bamboo cutting, felling of trees, catechu and charcoal making. The kathodis have different stages of cultural development according to their different occupations. They were brought to Rajasthan i.e. Udaipur district by the Bohra contractors for preparation of *Katha* from *Kher* tree. According to 1991 census they constitute 2,984 (1,498 males and 1,486 females) persons in the state of Rajasthan. According to the 1921 Census Report their population in the country was 80,820 persons.

Origin and History

According to Welling the Katkarias are the people of jungles, who have no land of their own, no fixed profession,; they are hunters, coal makers, gatherers and sellers of forest produce, fresh water fisherman, field labourers and agriculturists.

Robert Heine-Golden, Editor of *Bulletin of International Committee on Urgent Anthropological and Ethnological Research* No. 3, Viena 1960, lists the Kathodis among the primitive tribes of India.

Stephun Fush calls them a sub-section of the Bhills, Hadden and Kene call them Dravidian. J.V. Ferriera opines, "the katkarias still retained the trace of ancient stock from which they originally stemmed but they seem today to indicate a considerable intermixture."

The Kathodis are the people of the hills and low forest. They lead an unsettled nomadic life. They are experts and are known for their frugality and endurance.

At present the Kathodis inhabit Shahabad of Baran district. In Udiapur district they are living in Bodadar, Juda, Samija and Vas villages of Kotra tehsil and Maripur, Madra, Ambasa, Amavi and Daiya villages of Jhadol tehsil.

According to K.J. Save the Ketkari constitute only the bottom ring of the social ladder of the original tribes. The Kathodis are considered to be interior to some of the aboriginal tribes like Warlis, Dhodias, Dublas, Konkans and Kolis of

Maharashtra. In the same way they are treated as inferior to the Mina, Bhil and Garasia tribes of Rajasthan. They do not like to dine with the Kathodi's nor accept water from them.

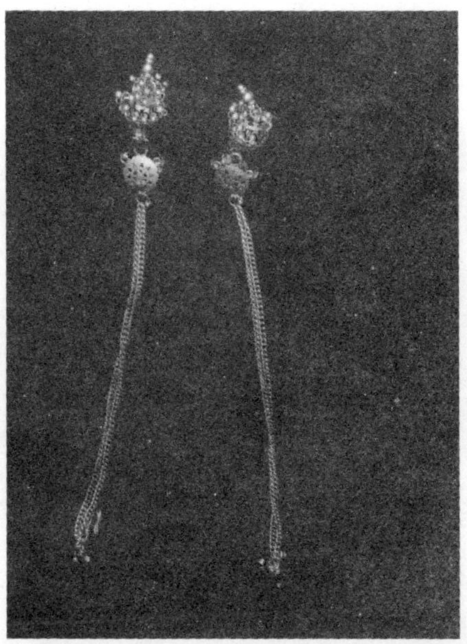

They are habituated to lead an unsettled nomadic life. Nomadism has become a cultural trait with the Kathodis. They are fond of wandering and can leave their habitations on the slightest encouragement. They are experts and are known for their frugality and endurance. They are fond of liquor and a major part of their earning is spend on drinking. The tribe is known as one of the most economically backward tribes of India. In Rajasthan their condition is more or less the same.

Kathodis have no role in the Indian history or in any struggle or reform movement.

Inhabitation

A Kathodi house has a typical appearance known as Kholra. It is of wood, grass and leaves. It is a wooden frame carved with grass and leaves. The roof is slanting on both sides. It is generally 4-5 feet high with a narrow, low entrance. It has no ventilation or windows. It is rectangular in shape. In front of the hut, generally a square shaped platform is raised and is used for keeping fodder and other things. The square platform rests on four wooden walls about 15 feet high hung in the air.

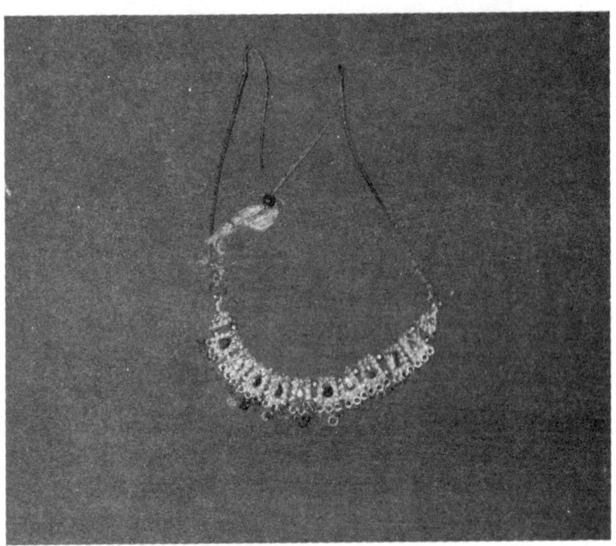

Clan

In Maharashtra the Kathodis are divided into two subsections, viz., Dhor Kathodi and Son Kathodi. The Dhor Kathodi is purely nomadic section and leads on unsettled life. In Maharashtra following exogamous clans can be seen Vardi Jangoda, Vaghira Nadagulyr, Bhenda, Pawar, Dhuma, Lakhan, Misal and Niwar.

The Kathodi clans are exogamous. The major clans are *Ketkar, Khopkar, Ahir, Bhopla.* The clan names are derived from territories and professions. In Rajasthan they observe many clans which are same as those of Bhils of the area in which they reside. Generally the following clans found viz. Chauhan, Singoda, Vagira, Nanama, Kharadi and Nadgiya.

The Kathodis are aware of *Varna* system and place themselves in the *sudra* category.

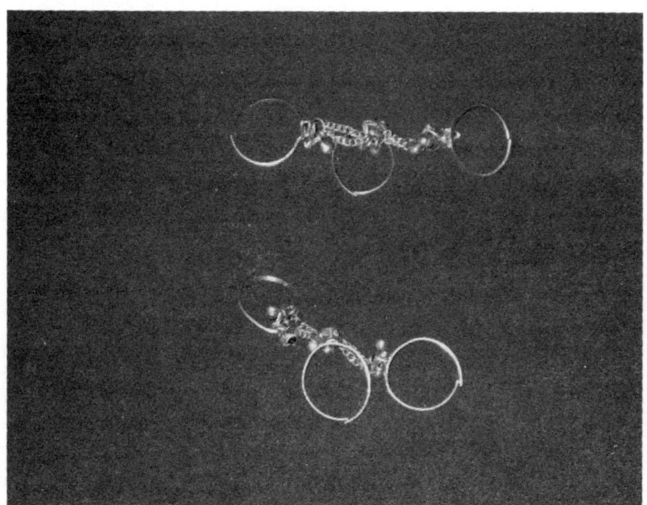

The study of clans among the Kathodis made by many anthropologist, reveals that some clans are totemistic, others are names of territories and few others refer to only profession, while some are the names of Maratha families another castes, like Ahir, Jangem, Kali, etc.

Family

Among the Kathodis the family is the unit of the social organisation. A Kathodi family is a self-centred family. It is common that the Kathodi groom, after marriage, joins the family of the father-in-law and live with him and cultivates his lands.

A Kathodi family is simple, nuclear, patriarchal in which the mate dominates over the female. The head of the family does not allow his wife to earn a living but his unmarried daughters are allowed to do so. However, the wife helps her husband by making bundles of the bamboos cut, and fetches brings them down from the hills. Likewise she works at home, but for wages as such she never works. The wives are loyal to their husbands. In Kathodis the family bond is strong and divorce can be seen in exceptional cases.

Birth: Customs related to birth are same for male and female child. Six day's pollution period is observed after the birth of a child. Mother and the child are confined to a hut for six days. Nobody is allowed to enter in that hut except mother-in-law and sister-in-law who look after the new born baby and mother. On the sixth day the mother is given purificatory bath. A ceremony called *Surya Puja* is also observed on twelfth day, on *Surya Puja* the mother and child took bath and worship the family deities. Tonsure ceremony is observed in six months.

Marriage: They are an endogamous community. Consanguinous marriages are prohibited. Junior sorrorate and levirate are permitted among them. Adult marriage is the rule now-a-days. The age of marriage is eighteen to twenty years for both boys and fourteen to sixteen for the girls.

Among the Kathodis marriage in the same *kul* is not permitted. They are exogamous. Divorce and widow marriage is allowed, but divorce can be seen in exceptional cases. The marriage of the son or daughter is decided by the parents. The father of the boy search a girl for his son. To settle the marriage, the father of the son goes to thc home of girl and settles the date of marriage. At the time of *Sagai* the brides father puts a redmark, *Tilak* or *Tika,* on the forehead of the bridegroom. A *dapa* or bride price fixed by the girls father is paid to the brides father by the bridegrooom. After the payment of *dapa*, the date of marriage is fixed. The bridegroom alongwith the *barat* starts for bride's house on the pre-arranged date. The marriage is celebrated by community dancing. Some *Hindu* rituals have been adopted by the Kathodis in their marriage ceremonies. A *mandap* is erected with the support of four *Saldi* tree sticks and covered by the leaves of *Jamun* tree. Under this *mandap* the marriage ceremony is performed, the burning fire being the witness. Just after marriage the bridegroom takes the bride to his house to receive the blessings of the parents and elder members of the family. The married boy then leaves the family of his parents and with his wife forms his own family.

Among the Kathodis a person prefers to marry the daughter of his mother's brother or daughter. This is only to observe strictly the clan custom at exogamy. Such practice is strictly prohibited in other tribal groups of the state of Rajasthan.

Widow marriage is performed in a very simple manner. In case of widow marriage bride price i.e. *dapa* is essential for it, if she do not marry with her *devar*.

Death: The Kathodi bury their dead, put liquor in the mouth of the corpse and place tobacco near it. After the death, the deceased is carried to the burial ground by the sons or nearest relatives. They put the soil over the dead body. The hut of the dead along with his belongings is set on fire. The Kathodi observe six days pollution period *gom* after the death of a person. During that period the sons or nearest relatives lead a simple life. The refrain from taking fish and meat.

After six days the relatives and friends assemble in the deceased house for drinking liquor. On festival days Kathodis perform *Kantiya ughodva* and place liquor and edibles on the grave i.e. burial ground.

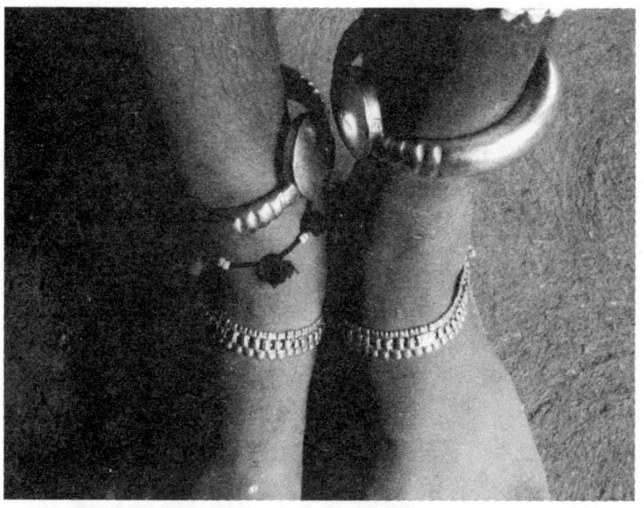

COSTUMES

The Kathodi's lives in very simple manner.

Male Costumes

The traditional Kathodi males used *langoti* as their wear. At later stage they use short *dhoti* covered a portion of the waist and upto thigh, leaving the rest of the body completely nacked. Now-a-days the Kathodi males wear *dhoti, kurta* and shirt. The young Kathodi also wear Pant. They use to wear *pagdi* or turban as a headdress. Many times they use *phata* on their head instead of *Pagdi.* Generally they wear red colour *pagadi* having length 3.5 metre and 16" width only. During the dance all the Kathodi male wear red *pagadi*, white *dhoti* and white *banayan* (white round neck sleeves vest). The school going children and youngsters wear nikkar, shirt, pant or T-shirt.

Female Costumes

The traditional Kathodi women dress is 9 metre long *sari* which they wear in a Maharashtrian pattern. Some of their female did not wear any cloth on their upper portion. Now-a-days the Kothdi women wear *ghaghra, patticoat, dhoti (sari), odhni, kanchli* and blouse. They prefer dark colours. The length of *sari* or *dhotis* 5 metre while the *odhni* having 1.5 metre length and one metre width. *Odhni* is worn by just tucked on to the head and both the ends were left open or sometimes tucked into the *ghaghra.*

The *ghaghra* with some shining *sitara* work or golden, silver thread embroidered were worn by the women. The bride generally wear red *ghaghra* with golden work. The school-going girls wear skirt & blouse, *kurta and pyjama* also.

Both male and female like to wear *chhaplas* in their feet.

Ornaments

The Kathodi males are fond of ornaments. They wear *chain* in the neck, *long* in the ear and *kada* in the wrist.

Kathodi females are very much fond of ornaments. They wear ornaments from head to toe. They wear *bor, tika* on head, *song* in noble, *tokari, tops* in ears, *chain, modlia* and *mangalsutra* in neck, *kada* and *churi* in hand or wrist, *viti or* ring in finger, *pajeb* in ankle and *bichhia* in toe. Generally their ornaments are made from gillet or any other material. They wear *long* only made by silver or gold. They also use bead ornaments like *mala,* earings etc.

Tattooing

Kathodi females preferred tattooing. They like to mark tattooing on forehead, neck, arms, legs, cheeks and chin. The common motifs are sun, moon, bird, peacock, name of person, dots, flowers etc. The man generally tottoo their name and any mark of their diety.

CHAPTER 8

Lushei Kuki

Dr. Prakash Chandra Mehta

The Lushei Kuki's reside between the Kurnaphuli river and its main tributory. The Tuilianpui on the west, and the Tyao and Koladyne river on the east, while their southern boundary is roughly a line drawn east and west through the junction of the Mat and Koladyne rivers and their most northerly villages are found on the borders of the Silchar district. Within this area, roughly 7,500 sq. miles, there are only a few villages ruled over by chiefs of other clans, and outside it there are but few true Lushei villages. On the southern borders of Sylhet in Tipperah and in the North Cachar Hills and they are a few in the Chittagong Hill tracts.

Clan

All the Lushei Kuki clans resemble each other very closely in appearance and the Mongolian type of countenance prevails. One meets, many exceptions, which may be due to the foreign blood introduced by the many captives taken from the plains and from neighbouring tribes, but these are not worth considering. The Lushai clans of both sexes are as a rule rather slighter made than among the Thado and Cognate clans.

Origin and History

The Lushai Kuki's claims that they are descendent from a certain Thang-ura, who is sometimes said to have spring from the union of Burman with a Paihte woman, but, according to the Paihtes, the Lushais are descendent from Boklus, an illegitimate son of Paihte Chief Ngehguka. The Thados say that some hunters tracking a serao noticed the foot-marks of a child following those of the animal, and on surrounding the doe serao they found it suckling a child, who become the great chief Thang-ura or, as they call him *Thangul*. From Thang-ura the pedigree of all the living chiefs fairly accurately established. The Lushais, in common with the Thados and other kuki tribes, attach great importance to their genealogies; and pedigrees, given at an interval of many years, and by persons living far apart, have been to agree this fact. From comparison of these genealogies and from careful enquiries lasting over many years. Thang-ura must have lived early in the eighteenth century. His first village is said to have been at Thangkua, north of Falam.

It is a probable that he personally ruled over only a small area. From him sprang six lines of Thang-ura chiefs viz Rokum, Zadeng, Thangluah, Pallian, Rivungand Salio. To the north the country was occupied by the Suket, Paihte and Thado clans. These appear to have been firmly established under regular chiefs; but to the west the hills appear to have been inhabited by small communities formed largely of blood relations and probably each at feud with its neighbours.

The Sailo chiefs are descended from Sailova, a great grandson of Thang-ura's. They came into prominance last, but have crushed all their rivals, and have developed such a talent from governing that they hold undisputed sway over representatives of all sorts of clans, over nearly the whole of the area now known as the Lushai Hills.

The various branches of the Sailo family were frequently at war, the cause almost invariably being a dispute as to land.

Later the Northern chiefs quarrelled among themselves, and the war of the East and West broke out and lasted several years. The cause is said to have been a girl called Tuali, for whose affections Liankhama and Khalkhama rivals. It is unnecessary to go into the history dealings with the Lushais, which have, ended in the whole of the Hills being annexed, and a stop put to all such wars, but when he occupied Lungleh in 1889 he found the Fanai clan coming into prominence, and there is little doubt that, but for intervention, that clan would shortly have attempted to eject the southern Lushai chiefs.

The Lushais are more or less closely allied to all the tribes now living in their vicinity, but some who show this most strongly, viz. Chiru, Kom, Aimol are now settled in the Manipur state, while the intervening country is occupied by clans belonging to the Thado, Paihte, and Khawtlang families, which, though no doubt the same stock, are more distantly connected. It seems certain that the former clans lived near the Lusheis when the Thangur commenced their victorious career, and it may well be that it was fear of absorption by their more powerful neighbour that drove these clans northwards, while Lusheis took a westerly direction.

COSTUMES

Male Costumes

The men's dress is pypical one. It is prepared by a 7 feet long and 5 feet wide cloth. It is worn as follows—one corner is grasped in the left hand, and the cloth is passed over the left shoulder, behind the back, under the right arm across the chest and the end thrown over the left shoulder. Although it would appear probable that clothing so loosely worn may be continually falling oft. In cold weather one or more clothes are worn, one over the other, and also a white coat, reaching well down the thigh but only fastened at the throat. These coats are ornamented on the sleeves with bands of red and white of various patterns. When at work, in hot weather, the Lushai wraps his cloth round the waist, letting the ends hang down in front. All these garments are of cotton, grown locally and manufactured by the women of the household. The clothes in general are white, but every man likes to have two or three blue clothes ornamented with strips of various colours.

In the rain Lushais wear hats made of strips of bamboo or cane plainted and lined with smoked leaves.

On special occasions or ceremony they wear dark blue clothes, with red lines of a particular pattern, and plumes, made of tail feathers of the king-crow, in their hair knots.

Female Costumes

The women are no more addicted to fine clothes than their men-folk. All women wear the same costume, a dark-blue cotton cloth, just long enough to go round the waist with a slight over lap and held by a girdle of brass wire or string, serves as a petticoat which only reaches to the knee, the only other garments being a short white jacket and a cloth which is worn in the same manner as the man. On gala days the only addition to the dress in a picturesque head-dress worn by the girls. This is made by a porcupine quills, and to the upper ends of these are fixed by the green wing-feathers of the parrot, tipped with tufts of red wool. At the back is affixed a horizontal bar from which hang strings of glistening wing covers of green beetels.

Tattooing

Tattooting is not much practised. The only patterns employed are circles on the forearm and breast, which are said to be momentoes of love affairs in happy bachelor days.

Ornaments

The Lushai wears a variety of ornaments in their hair knot. The most common is a brass two-pronged pin with head shaped like a G. The prongs are drawn out to a sharp points and vary in length from three to mine inches. These very long pins are new, and their use is restricted to the young *dandies* of hamlets round Aizal. Skewers of ivory, bone and metal about six or eight inches are also used. Of the two former there are two patterns, one four-sided, about a quarter of an inch thick at two-third of its length, tapering to a point at each end, the being flat, pointed at one end and about half an inch broad at the other end. Both are ornamented. They wear necklaces of very amber and beads. Besides the amber, agate, corneliam and various sorts of bead necklaces are worn by them. They also use white shirt buttons. Both sexes are found of necklaces.

A tiger's tooth is often wear in the neck as an ornament and is also thought that it bears magical properties. The young dandies are fond of hanging round their necks tufts of white goat's hair bound together with red thread, these are used as ornament.

Bracelets are not much popular and they generally wear plain brass rings.

The Lushai women affect the same ornaments as the man. The earrings, however, are quite distinct, and, in order to be able to wear them, special preparation is necessary. When quite a child girl has her ears pierced, and small wooden plugs are inserted. These are replaced by larger ones, by this way the size of which is gradually increased till the real earning, which is an ivory disc some inch or inch and a half in diameter, with a hole in its centre. Widows remove their earrings and slit the lobes of their ears when they abandon all thought of re-marrying.

CHAPTER 9

Mina

Dr. Prakash Chandra Mehta

Mina is the dominant tribal group of Rajasthan. According to 1991 census their strength was 27,99,167 (1,469,158 males and 1,330,009 females) persons, they constitute about 50 per cent of the total tribal population of the state. The Minas who ruled over some of the *Jagirs* and *Thikanas* of the former states of Jaipur and Alwar are basically an agricultural community. Their concentration is mainly in the eastern part of the Rajasthan i.e. Jaipur, Sawai-Madhopura Karauli, Dausa and Alwar. Though, they are also found in the districts of Udaipur, Chittorgarh, Kota, Bundi, Tonk and Dungarpur. Out of the total Mina population more than half reside in the districts of Jaipur, Sawai-Madhopur, Karaali, Dausa and Udaipur. In Rajasthan they are declared in the list of scheduled tribe, while in Uttar Pradesh, Madhya Pradesh, Haryana and Punjab they are covered under general category.

As a major tribal group the development programmes for the Minas are implemented through the Modified Area Development Agency (MADA).

In Uttar Pradesh they are known as *Pardeshi Rajput,* in Madhya Pradesh they are called by the name *Rawat.*

Origin

Mina trace their origin in a number of myths, legends and oral anecdotes. Although the derivation of the word Mina

(Meena) is obscure, it has been suggested that it means fish. It is found that the Minas consider fish as a taboo. A alluding to a mythology, they trace their origin to *Matsay* or *Minavatar* the tenth incarnation of Lord Vishnu in the disguise of fish. References to Mina are also found in *Matsya Puran.*

The origin, thus, is related to Vishnu, one of the trinities of Hindu gods.

History

No systematic history of the antiquity of Minas has been written. However, there are references of the tribe which go back to 500 B.C. The Minas has their encounters with *Rajput* rulers right from 12th century onwards. Minas were associated with the rulers of Amber. The history obviously shows that all through the 12th century, the struggle between Minas and Rajputs was continuous affair. The result of the struggle was that the Rajputs succeeded in establishing their hegemony over the Minas. Minas missed no opportunity in giving rise to one upheavel or the other. By committing some act of plunder and theft they continued to create problems of law and order.

At the later stages of social formation the Minas were obliged by the Rajputs to take a settled way of life. The Minas on their part also accepted agriculture as their main source of livelihood.

Inhabitation

The smallest unit of settlement of Minas is the *Dhani,* which in the Bhil area known as *Falan. Dhani,* therefore, is a patrilineal group which has an identified ancestor and generally it's name is after the founder ancestor. A number of *Dhanies* constitute a village. *Dhani* is strictly an exogamous group. Non-Minas are not allowed to reside in the *Mina Dhani.* In some villages the smallest *Dhani* has two houses and the largest *Dhani* may have 10-15 houses.

The Minas reside in compact villages. The area of a village has well marked boundaries. The Minas reside with other caste groups in a village. Their fields are at some distance from the village. They do not live in scattered villages like other tribal groups. The Mina village, in all its aspects, needs an infrastructures conform to the general pattern of villages which is compact.

The typical Mina house is made of mud walls and thatched roots. The central part of the house is partitioned by thick mud walls with only one entrance. This area enclose the main courtyard and the living rooms. The kitchens are made adjacent to the respective rooms under thatched roof. Now-a-days the Mina's are living in *Kuchha-Pucca* and *Fully Pucca* houses with all the amenities which they can afford. They store their animals' fodder in a special type of house known as *Top.* Generally they use *Kande* (dry cow/buffalo dung cake) as a fuel. Minas generally tie their animal near their house in a courtyard.

Clan

Generally one clan people lives in a village but in a big village more than one clan Minas reside. The clans plays an important role in their marital relations. Minas clans are generally resemble to *Rajput* clans. The popular clans are Chauhan, Parmar, Gahlot, Kachhawa, Yadav, Tanvar, Padihar, Nirwan, Gaur, Badgujar, Solanki, etc.

In Minas, those who do not eat cow and ox meat known as *Ujala Mina* and meat eaters are *Maila Mina*. It is believed that *Dhudan* area Minas are *Ujala* and rest area Minas are *Maila* Mina. There are many myth/related to their *Gotrs* (clan) and their reknowned persons of the society have quoted a number of *Gotras* in their literature.

Family

The Minas prefer joint family. In their family married sons lived with parents. They do not like to separate their sons after marriage. They live together in a single courtyard. If any shortage of accommodation, they construct more rooms in the same courtyard. Mina named their family *Kutumb.* In minas child marriage is prevalent, but the bride remains at her fathers house till *Gauna.* Father is the head of family. After the death of father, the eldest son will be the head of family. All the family member pay due respect to the head of family and consult him in important matters.

Life-Cycle

Birth: Generally birth takes place at the husband's house. The functions of delivery are performed by the elderly women of the community. On the birth of boy they beat *thali* (brass-plate), if it is girl beat winnowing fan (*Sup*). The period of confinement observe, upto the day of *nahan* (bath) which varies from 6 to 27 days. On the day of *chota nahan bhuwa* draws a swastic sign on the outer wall of room in which the birth takes place. On the day of *bara nahan,* the ceremony of *Kua Poojan* takes place. They also observe naming and *mundan* ceremony.

Marriage: The Minas are also an endogamous group. They are exogamous too. Exogamy is practised within his own *gotra*. The marriagable age in Minas for boy is 12-14 years and in the case of girl it is 10-12 years. The marriage is settled among them by the parents. In this tribal group bride price is not taken, while dowry is prevalent among the Minas. The first ritual of marriage is *Sagai*–takes place on some auspicious day and *tika* from the girls side in sent to the side of boy. Mina observe all the rituals of marriage as *Hindu* observes at boy and girls house. The marriage ceremony is performed by *Brahmin.* Generally the bride is immature, *gauna* ceremony is performed after one, three or seven years. Mina is a Monoganous tribal group.

Widow marriage is permitted among the Mina. Generally a widow preferred to marry with her *Devar* i.e. younger brother of deceased husband. This type of marriage is celebrated in a simple manner.

Divorce is permissible in the Minas. The men mainly seek divorce on the ground of adultry, sterility, incurable diseases and negligence of duties towards husband and children. The women can also seek divorce. However in practice the cases of divorce are very few. There is no re-payment of ornaments or gifts given to the bride's father in the case of divorce. On the other hand if woman wants to divorce her husband demands a cash compensation from the wife's father.

Nata marriage is also observed in the Minas. In this marriage, a married women with living husband and offsprings can re-marry another married man–her second husband paying a cash compensation known as *Jhagra* which is prevalent among all the tribal groups. And in several cases the woman's father and her-in-laws claim the *Jhagra.* In the *nata* marriage only simple rituals are observed. The *Brahmin* perform this marriage ceremony with simple rituals.

Death

Funeral ceremony among the Mina is almost similar to the Hindus. Dead body of child is created on the third day, the bones and ashes are collected by the nearest relatives known as *Phool* are sent to be immersed in the *Ganges* or into some holly water. On the 12th day, a feast is given, and in case the deceased was a head male person, a turban is tied to the eldest son to mark the transfer of the headship of the family. After six months and also after a year *barsi* ceremony is performed with a feast.

COSTUMES

The Mina costume is some way different from other tribal groups.

Male Costumes

The male Meena generally wear *dhoti, kurta, bandi* and *Safa (*turban*).* The younger generation wear pant, jeans, shirt and T-shirt also. School-going children use shirts and shorts. During winter season male use shawl or *chadar* for covering upper part of the body.

Female Costumes

The dress of women consists of *ghaghra, odhni, kanchali* and *kurti.* They generally use dyed red or yellow colour *odhani.* Now-a-days the young generation also wear *sari, blouse* and *petticoat.* Their *ghaghra* is usually made of dark red cloth with blue designs. The colour of *ghaghra* is of bright crimson profusely stitched with laces. Unmarried girls wear *saries* called *loogada* of fast colour without laces.

The costumes of Minas of southern Rajasthan is resembles with the costumes of Bhils.

Ornaments

Mina males use very few ornaments. In ears they wear *murki* (earrings) and *kada* in their wrist.

The women are very much fond of ornaments like the tribal women. On the forehead they use *borla.* It is indication that the women is married and her husband is alive. Besides *borla*, the women wear *hansli, chain* round the necke, *kanta* in the nose, *timnia* in the ear, poonchi, *bangdi, gajora churi* on the forearms and *bajuband* on the upper arm. Married women generally wear *churas* which is made from *lac.*

Tattooing

Men and women both get tattooing on their body. Men have their names, figures of their deity on their arms. Women get tattooed on their hands and cheeks. The most common designs viz. dots, flowers and name of the person.

By this way the mina tribal group has special indentity regarding the costumes like other tribal groups of the country.

CHAPTER 10

Oraon

Dr. Nabakumar Duary

Chotanagpur plateau of Jharkhand is a tribal concentrated area, where exist many tribal groups. They have distinct identity in language, traditional culture and customs. Some of them are traditionally known as artisan groups on the basis of age-old occupation. The Oraon are of the important settled agriculturist Dravidian tribal group of Chotanagpur. The earlier studies reported that Kankan was the original homeland of the Oraon. They are migrated from the west coast of India towards north India through river valley and settled down as agriculturist and land-owners in the Shahabad district of the then Bihar and from there, they further driven to Rohtasgarh and lastly entered into the then Munda area of Chotanagpur in centuries ago (Roy 1984 and Gupta 1974). The Oraons are belonging to the Sarna religion. But some of them followed Christianity during the British period (Sahay 1976, Sahay and Duary 1998, Duary 1999). They are living with different tribal groups including artisan tribes like Chick Baraik (weaver), *Lohar* (blacksmith) and some artisan castes like *Sonar* (goldsmith), *Lohar* and *Gouria* (blacksmith), *Gaderiya* (shepherd), *Malhar* (metal craftsman as well as tattoo maker), *Kumhar* (potter), *Mochi* (cobbler), etc. These people are interacting with each other in different sphere of life. The Chick Baraik mainly supplies some unique types of dress materials to the Oraon. The Oraon purchase the dress materials from Chick Baraik from the village *hats* and from fairs. For tattooing and ornaments they are traditionally depending on *Malhar, Gouria*, goldsmith and blacksmith castes. They collect *bagirka* or wooden/ bamboo comb from Turi community and purchase looking glass or *aina* from the *hat* or from the fair. The *essung* or oil of *lakarkussa/karanj* is supplied by traditional oil crasher caste *Teli*, locally called Shaw (surname of the caste).

Dancers in Murmajatra

Traditionally, for cleaning of hair and protection from dandruff they use a typical type of dry clay called *nagra khanj* or *mati,* which is available in some particular places in surrounding areas. It is collect by female folk during the month of March- April and are stored it for a yearlong. Before using the *nagra khanj,* the user at first immerses it in water for making semi liquid nature. This tribal people use the *lakarkussa/karanj essung (Pongamia glabrd)* on hair and body for good health of hair, for protection from itching of skin during wet cultivation of paddy in rainy season and use it during winter for protection from dryness. The flowers, leaves, cockquills and palm leaves called *bakka pencha* and hairpin *khonges* during the performance of different kinds of traditional dances. The married women use the vermilion on head as marriage symbol. They use raincoat called *chhupi* or *ghungu,* made up of leaves of *ghungu* creeper and also use bamboo umbrella called *chhata.* These are used in rainy season for protection from rain during agriculture operation as well and also for protection from heat in summer.

Ritual Performance in Traditional Dress

COSTUMES

The costumes and body decoration is of the very age-old culture since prehistoric period. From the early evidences the people of Stone Age used the flower, foliage, colourful wings of insects, feathers of birds, coloured soil, stones and other objects for decoration of body. However, they also wear biotic parts of animal of different size and shape like bone, teeth, claws, shells, etc. They employed simple technology for shaping and joining each other with thread of barks or twigs. In later period i.e. during Neolithic age they invented the weaving. Apart from natural shelter in rock, they had constructed dwelling, wheel, made pottery, cultivation and domesticated animals.

Man wear the dress, ornaments and decorate their body with colour, clay, tattooing and other materials and projects the hairstyle not only the effect of physical environment but also for their own satisfaction and as well as to display for public through symbols. Such identification and interpretation of symbols give the specific cultural context (Westernmarck: 1930). In India these practices are very much reflected in almost all simple societies.

Performing Khaddi Dance with Traditional Dress in Ranchi Town

India is a plural society in terms of language, culture, tradition, economy, belief system including costumes and body decoration, from which it reflects the ethnic or community identity in different ecological and environmental setup. It is not alike in caste or tribal societies in India; rather it is more distinct than the caste societies. The tribal people collect some objects like seed, bark, jute, grass, leave, flower, wood and also clay, stone, glass beads, metal, teeth, bone, claws of animals and use these as ornaments. Some tribal societies practise various crafts including weaving for supplementing their livelihood. Though some of these serve their own purpose, yet their main objective is to earn money by selling them in the nearby markets.

Some tribal societies have uniqueness in many ways including dress, ornaments and body decoration. The present study is focussed on the traditional and contemporary costumes of the Oraon people in rural Chotanagpur and on the basis of age and gender in different occasion including daily life. The study has been done among the Oraons in Sosai; a multi-ethnic village in Mander block in Ranchi district of Jharkhand.

The *Pahan* on shoulder in Traditional Dress in *Murmajatra*

Both the genders of Oraon society wear different types of dress ornaments and they decorate their bodies and hairs in different occasion as well as in daily life. They wear various kinds of costumes during participation in different occasion like lifecycle rituals, religious performances, or at the time of *jatra/mela* or fairs/festivals e.g. *Khutajatra* or *Murmajatra, Parhajatra, Jagannathpur mela,* etc. They wear different types of dress and ornaments during recreation purposes and various types of *nalnas* or dances namely *Khaddi, Karam, Paiki* and war dance are performed in their courtyard. During marriage, the bridegroom party perform the *Paiki* dance at *Akhra* (village meeting place) for well-coming the groom party. The male dancers wear colourful and typical designed dresses. The Oraon people also wear different types of dress at the time of domestic and economic activities accordingly.

In earlier, the Oraon boys and girls wear small *karea* and *putli* (an old cotton piece) respectively. The unmarried girl wears *gaji.* They wear cowries on neck to avoid the evil eye and also use one kind of bangle called *kheadbalal* or *painara* in ankle for the said purpose.

The traditional male dresses of the Oraon are like *kareya, kadhani, gamcha, chadar* or *pechhouri, patwa* and *barkhi.* The adult female dresses are like *khanria, sari, thafra, pudhna* and *bathra gamcha.* These are made up of cotton thread and use regularly as well as during their traditional social and religious occasions.

One interesting fact is that the women folk of Oraon society celebrate the *Janisikar* every after twelve years interval in the memory of a war against the Mughal. The females wear male dress, put the turban or headgear, wear sunglass along with beard from the day of *Khaddi* or *Sarhul* festival and start hunting expedition the wild games in the local areas for a fortnight.

The male Oraon wears a typical type of dress and performs the dance in *Murmajatra* and the *Parhaparav* and wears traditional dress and decorated himself with flowers and feathers. The details of costumes used by male and female is given below:

Karya-is a long cotton cloth (length is about 6 ft-7 ft.), which covered the lower part of the body.

Kadhani-a cotton rope on waist as supporting the *karya* or a girdle.

Gamacha- used daily at the time of bath as well as for keeping on shoulder during journey towards *hat* for carrying daily commodities. It has also multipurpose use.

Chadar- is a long white cotton cloth with red border, used in winter and in marriage ceremony.

Patoas- these are the colour belts with different sizes, used by the boys and adult males on heads as headgear. These are made by *kasi* grasses or *khejur* palm leaves. The structure is like a crown and worn at the time of *jatra.*

Saree-only adult female wears it. In earlier days the Chick Baraik supplied it.

Thafra- in earlier the female wear it on waist.

Bathragamacha- it is a white cotton long cloth, with red borders and with some geometric designs, which reflect some motives. Mother mainly uses this for carrying baby on shoulder (length 7 ft. and width 2.5 ft.).

Ornaments

The male and female wear different kind of ornaments in many parts of their bodies and these are made up of various kinds of materials. The womenfolk used the brass metal ornaments in legs, arms, hands, fingers, toes, ears, anklets and necks. The Oraon bride wear *painra* (anklet), in her marriage, gifted by her parents along with all sorts of ornaments namely *bala* or bracelets, *rasnia* or thick brass bracelet, *hansli (solid* brass crescent shaped necklace), *chandoamala* or necklaces made up of silver coins strung together.

The earring is called *muddi* and is made up of silver. The right septum of the nose pin made up of silver is called *nagmuktri.* After the age of 45 years, *nagmuktri* replaced by silver ornaments known as *besar.* The female wears three kind of earring on upper part, middle part and on lop area of ear. The names of these ornaments are called *jhika, bijkanai* and *bindo* respectively. However, they wear different types of rings which have separate names on the basis of material used and where they wear on the bodies e.g. *lohamuddi* or *khongso / jhutia* in toe (iron), *gouriamuddi* in finger (brass), *sonarmuddi* in hand (gold), *jhutia* in toe (brass).

Sometimes they use the palm leaf rolled up with lac ring called *tarbindio* and stem of *bazra* or *gangai* plants for said purpose and is called *gangai bindo.*

During festival time the adult female use the *mathia* or bangle (silver) in both hands and also use iron bangles called *luhabala* for protection from ghost.

The female wear different kinds of silver ornaments in three levels on the neck like *khambia, chandwa* (just below the neck), *sikrdi* or chain (middle row) and *hansli* (last row).

The woman also wears *bainkal* or *bijait* (brass) just below the elbow.

The female also wear the hand-made grass ornaments on neck namely *phutchirapoon, kaiskodaipoon* and *kachpoon.* Moreover, they also use the china beads called *mocharpoon.* Other ornaments of the female were like *tarkala parpat (ear-plugs* of rolled up painted string), *rita mala* (necklace), *mala (*necklace with long woollen string), *tainri* (solid brass ring for ankles), *dori (*woollen string with tassels to tie women's hair into a knot), *thotiya* (4 thick brass rings for toes with 2 copper wires for fastering them on to the toes).

In earlier, the grass necklace of the young Oraon male was received as presentation or gift from a young girl to whom he is attached. The male wears the iron bracelet called *panabera* or iron finger ring for protection from harmful lightning. This is not like an ornament but it is a special kind of thing, which is made up of iron, and has been exposed to the open sky during an eclipse of the sun or of the moon. People who are born with the fact forward are believed to be particularly liable to lightning strokes and so it is much person who generally...........(Roy 1984: 63). In marriage ceremony and in *jatra* the young inserts a few porcupine quills *(surahi chaour)* into his waist girdle and back of the waist and one on each side. The male folk wear *muddi* or finger ring and *lurka* or earring and wear *chilpi tayna* (brass ring worn on the forehead to keep their hairs in place, *kardani* (belt of leather strings worn by men). The boy wears the earring *lurka* after the performance of ear perforation ceremony at the age of 7-8 years, which is called *kanchhandi.* This ceremony is performed in presence of kin, clan and family members.

Tattooing

The tattooing is one identification mark for the Oraon female and by which they are easily identified from other neighbouring ethnic groups. There are some folk tales, which are associated to their migration from Rohtashgarh to present area during Mughal empire. Generally they make tattooing in the childhood. In this work the specialised professional women use mainly the iron needles, pigment powder, charcoal and oil. The impressions are made on forehead, arms, neck and neck region, chest and legs according to the choice of the subject and capacity of payment of remuneration. There is no such belief to evil and cure of disease. But in earlier, some aged person practise it for coming out the dead blood, which is to be cure method of relieving the pain of lower and upper limbs. The Oraon people often stated that after death all ornaments might be taken out from the body but tattooing is not taken off at death, and they carry with them to the next world.

REFERENCES

1. Duary, Nabakumar (1999): Oraon Dances in Chotanagpur: An Impact Study, *Tribal Dances of India,* Eds. Robin D. Tribhuwan and Preeti R. Tribhiwan, Discovery Publishing House, New Delhi.
2. Duary, Nabakumar and Sudhansu Shekhar Mahato (2003-2004): Some Traditional Customs among the Oraons of Chotanagpur Plateau, *Bulletin of the International Committee on Urgent Anthropological and Ethnological Research,* No. 42-43.

3. Gupta, Sattya Prakash (1974): *'Tribes of Chotanagpur Plattau: An Thnɔ-Nutritional & Pharmacological Cross-Section,* Bihar Tribal Welfare Research Institute, Ranchi.

4. Roy, S. C. (1984): *The Oraons of Chotanagpur,* Man in India Office, Catholic Press, Ranchi (first published in 1915).

5. Sachchidananda (1964): *Culture Change in tribal Bihar: Munda and Oraon,* Bookland Private Limited, Calcutta.

6. Sahay, K. N. (l976): *Under the Shadow of the Cross,* Institute of Social Research and Applied Anthropology, Calcutta.

7. Sahay, Vijoy. S. and Nabakumar Duary (1998): The Fading Traditional Tribal Institutions of Chotanagpur: A Study of the Oraons and Mundas, *Vanyajati,*Vol.XLVI, No.4.

8. Singh, K. S. (1984): The *Scheduled Tribes, People of India,* Anthropological Survey of India, Vol. III, Oxford University Press, Calcutta.

9. Westernmarck, Edward A. (1930): *Wit and Wisdom in Morocco: A study of Native Proverbs,* London, Routledge.

CHAPTER 11

Pahari Korwa

Dr. Prakash Chandra Mehta

The tribe Pahari Korwa is a branch of Mundas of Chotanagpur, which forms one of the main centre in India of aboriginal tribes. In other words, they are Munda branch of Astro-Asiatic sub-family of Austric family. Colonel Dalton in his descriptive ethnology of Bengal has written that Pahari Korwas are the dropped links of the Calarian chains. It is said that Pahari Korwas moved westward into Kudia region of Jashpur state (at present Jashpur district is in Chhattisgarh state) from Chotanagpur. From Khudia, in due course of time, they further migrated to the adjoining region of the Surguja state and settled in Surguja (district of Chhattisgarh state) at Ratanpur Betkuli. From Surguja a group of them migrated Palamau highlands (Bihar state) and further in the hills of Vindyachal near Dhudhi, Mirzapur distirct of Uttar Pradesh.

In Khudia region of Jaspur state, Pahari Korwa settled down in the dense forests and started living by *Jhuming* (shifting cultivation). They were concentrated only with their own immediate needs and protections and exercised their rights only for safety. They claimed forests, become their abode, the native place. They claimed that they are descendent from *Kudia Rai* (a deity i.e. *devi*) and Khudia is their native place.

Pahari Korwa are living in the village, each homestead of their used to have its home perched away in some accessible spot on the hillside. They had been always wild and dangerous to people with whom they came into contact. Since their early days they were dependent on hunting and shifting cultivation. The present socio-economic condition of the tribe reveal that they are not at the early stage of culture, but still away from the pastoral stage. They have their own rich cultural heritage.

Origin

About the origin of this tribal group no specific literature is available which could through light on the origin of this tribal group. Only one mythological story tells us about their origin. The story is narrated as under:

Once upon a time, Lord Mahadeo and Goddess Parvati sown the paddy after burning a patch of forest called *Daahi* in the Korwa dialect. To protect the paddy from wild animals. Mahadeo made a statue of a man and placed with muddy soil and put bow and arrow in his both the hands and placed him in the middle of the field. After this they marched ahead to their destination. When the time for harvest came, they returned to their paddy field and became happy to watch the paddy intact. No damage had been done to the crop by the wild animals. Paddy was harvested. The Parvati requested Mahadeo to give life to that mud statue made by him to watch the field. Mahadeo told Parvati that if life had been given to the statue, he would kill every one with his bow and arrow and eat, but Parvati insisted and compelled him to do so. So Mahadeo blew life in that statue and that mud man stood before them alive, with bow and arrow in his hands. The Lord said to him "You have protected my field from wild animals and producing the sound ko-rava-ko-rava" so your name would be Korwa, go and live in forest.

By this way, the name Korwa came into existence and the progeny of the Korwa constituted the tribal group called

Korwa. Since then the Korwa were doing: *Daahi* i.e. burning the forests, sprickle the seeds of paddy and started shifting cultivation for their livelihood. When the ancestors of Korwas were forced to stop the practice of *Dadhi* and shifting cultivation; to observe this age old tradition, before sowing the field, they did *Dadhi* by collecting leaves and bushes in the middle of the field in a small area and *Siru* the heap of leaves just to maintain the tradition given to them by Lord Mahadeo. It is their belief that Mahadeo would sow their field after *Daahi* therefore, they also did *Daahi* for *Shagun* (omen).

Clan

The tradition as well as philological and cultural evidences have shown that Korwas of Khudia region are divided in their social life into two groups long-long ago and named them Dehari Korwa and Pahari Korwa. Further, in their social life Deharia Korwas is divided into three sub-groups viz. Dewanihar, Dhanuhar or Nartorwa, and Majhi. Among these Dewanihar Korwas came in contact other tribes and soon process of took place among them and in comparison to remaining two i.e. Dhanuhar and Majhi Korwas, they became more civilized and respectable.

Dhanuhar-Korwas are also called *Nortorwa* or *Rehala* because they have adopted different social customs related to child-birth. They cut the umbilical cord with their own hands (without the help of knife but twist and break) after the delivery of a child. So they are called *Nartorwa.* In social hierarchy, after Dewanihar, Dhanuhar come and then Majhi. Dewanihar korwas do not give their daughters to Dhanuhar and Majhi Korwas i.e. they do not marry with them, but take their daughters. Dahnuhar and majhi Korwas establish marital relations between themselves.

Among all these clans of Deharia Korwas, Dewanihar Korwas are less in number and there population is concentrated and confined to few villages.

Dialect

The mother tongue of Korwas is called *Korwai,* it is a dialect. The *Korwai* is strictly spoken by Pahari Korwas. Dehari Korwas do not speak *Korwai.* Kodak tribe, who are probably the descendants of Korwas, also speak *Korwai.* The *Korwai* is very close to *Asuri* and resembles with *Mundari* and *Santhali* dialects.

COSTUMES

In general it is observed and found that Pahari Korwas are short of clothes i.e. minimum clothes have been found on their body of both the sexes.

Children below the age of six of both the sexes are found nacked in their daily life. Hardly the child covers the lower part of the body. Children, more than six, use shorts or *langoti* to covering the lower part of the body.

Male Costumes

Pahari Korwa males wear short white *dhoti* upto knee or use *langoti* to hide their lower portion of the body. *Langoti* is a thin strip of cloth about 9" wide and a yard long. This is passed between the thigh and attached by the ends to a waist string. Mostly, the upper part of body is naked. Shirts and ganji are luxury to them. In winter they cover upper portion with white cotton *chadar.* It is two to three yards in length and about one and a half yard in breadth. An average male is satisfied with a *dhoti* and a shirt or *ganzi.* All the clothes used by them are made by course cotton.

Female Costumes

Female wears short white cotton *dhoti,* 5 ft. in length to cover the whole body. Blouse and inner garments are common part of their dress. Mostly, under *dhoti,* upper half of the body is nacked. Hardly they wear blouse or bra. Generally female wear *dhoti* and a piece of cloth to use as a petticoat or long piece of cloth to use as *langoti.* All the clothes used or wear by the females are made of cotton course cloth vize Sari *(dhoti), langoti,* blouse/jacket, *ghaghra, chaddar* and *jhula* (loose blouse) are the main clothes used by the females.

ORNAMENTS

Male Ornaments

The male are not very much fond of ornaments. So, wearing of ornament is an option for them. Generally male use to wear *Gotimala* and *Mungamala* around their neck. They also wear brass or German silver rings in both the wrists and German silver rings in the middle or forefinger. To prepare a *Gotimala,* small piece of round metal is tied in a twisted thick-thread. *Mungamala* is made by small red coloured *Munga* beads, interwoven in a twisted thick yarn.

Female Ornaments

The females are very much fond of ornaments. They generally wear *Mungamala* (necklace), *Bera* (Bracelet), *Paire* (Anklet), *Nakhuti* (nose-pin), *Jhotis* or *Biehia* (toe rings) and earrings. *Mungamala* is worn around the neck, *Bera* is adorn on both the wrists, *Parie* is worn in both legs. Nakhuti is worn in nose. *Jhutia* is worn in the mdidle toes of both the legs and *Terkula* is worn in the ear-lobes. Imitation coin necklace made of German silver is also worn by the females. They also wear *Thosa* made from aluminimum and beads and *Hansuli* made from German silver and *Suta* are the forms of necklaces.

At the age of five or six years, Pahari Korwa girls gets the septum of her nose and both her ear-lobes are bored and a reed is inserted in all the holes. The boring of nose and both ear lobes are carried at home by the *mama.* In similar manner the ear-lobes of boys are also bored and reed inserted. Glass bangles and *Bera* are given to girls at the age of five or six years.

The young girls, before marriage can wear ornaments. There is no restrictions. It depends upon the economic condition of the family of the girl. Before marriage and after marriage, females give much preference to all kinds of ornaments like *Terkula, Bera, Nakhuti* and different types of necklaces.

Tattooing

Tattooing among Pahari Korwas is simply a mark of decoration. It is found in male and female both. Tattooing in males is called *Dhraha,* it is only marked in the childhood in both the hands above the wrist. When a boy attained the age of four or five *Dharha* is done.

Tattooing in females is done on any part of the body, where they use ornaments. Thus tattooing is carried on both the wrists, around the neck, chest, legs and ankle with different type of marks. Tattooing is not done on forehead, and back on the body. Generally the length of tattooing on the wrist is nearly six inches and legs above ankles is nearly four inches is done. The female are very much pond of tattooing.

CHAPTER 12

Saharia

Dr. Prakash Chandra Mehta

Saharia is the only primitive tribal group of Rajasthan. The Saharia are also pronounced as *Seharia, Sehria* and *Sahariya.* According to 1991 census they constitute 59,810 (30,555 males and 29,255 females) and constitute about one per cent of the tribal population. A majority of them lives in the Sahabad and Kishanganj tehsils of Baran district. The Saharia can be seen in Jhalawar, Udaipur, Dungarpur, Sawai-Mathopur, Jaipur and Bharatpur districts. They are believed to have been the Bhils once upon a time. Before, independence, the Saharias were bought and sold like chattels and were treated as slaves. Unaware of settled life, the practiced zoom *(Dahi)* i.e. shifting cultivation. Living in isolated dense forests, they become extremely shy by nature.

Origin

The Muslim rulers of Sahabad perhaps gave them their present name. *Sehr* in Persian means *jungle* and since these people lived in the *jungle* they come to be called *Saharias* also lived in neighbouring districts of Madhya Pradesh viz. Morena, Gwalior, Shivpuri and Guna.

History

There is very little mention of Saharia in the medieval history of Rajasthan. Col. Jumes Tod has made certain observations about this group which was living in the Sahabad and

Kishanganj of erstwhile Kota state and Morena, Gwalior, Shivpuri and Guna of the Central India.

Inhabitation

The Saharias are living in scattered villages. Their fields are away from their houses. However, the hamlets are slightly far off from the main villages. Each village has a cluster of Saharia families in a separate hamlet known as *Saharana.* In the *Saharana* no other caste people live. In the centre of each *Saharana* they construct umbrella type shelter house which is named *Bungalow,* where all Saharias sit together to discuss, gossip and settle their disputes. Shoes are not allowed in *Bungalow*. Women are also forbidden from entering the hall.

The houses constructed by the Saharias consist of mud and thatched roofs. These houses do not have any sanitation facilities and no proper ventilation. Till today they prefer to live in their age old pattern houses.

Clan

Saharia is an endogamous tribe divided into number of clans. Each clan named after some ancestor or place to which they originally belong. The important clans are Bedgor, Bhilodiya, Chackrya, Chowdarya, Dediya, Devaria, Garwar, Gogaya, Haleriya, Jaswariya, Kuhar, Kheti, Khanwar, Khadiya, Kaluaj, Mogriya, Navriya, Parenatia, Pateja, Rajouriya, Rewar, Ragpita, Chohan, Rathwar, Silwar Solvia and Solanki, etc.

Family

Saharia is an endogamous tribe but each clan in it is exogamous. They believe in totem and taboos and observe them during rituals and ceremonies. Like Bhils they also prefer nuclear family. Consists of husband, wife and unmarried children. When the eldest son gets married, he is asked to erect his own hutment within the enclosure of the ancestral house. The father also provide him a piece of land for his survival. The property of father is divided equally among the sons.

Life-Cycle

Birth: customs related to birth are same for male and female child. Generally the sweepress perform the delivery. Just after the birth of a child, a messanger is sent to girl's parents with sweets. On the third or fifth day after the delivery the mother and child are given a bath and taken out of the house for purification ritual known as *Bahar Nikalana.*

After the delivery, the mother is given jaggery and *mahua* water. During the maternity period, the mother fed on *dalia* prepared from jaggery and wheat or *jawar* flour. The collective pollution period is observed for three days during which contact with outsiders is forbidden after which the house is sacralised with cow dung. They observe naming ceremony on the purification day. On this day sweet balls are distributed and girl's parents bring clothes. Saharia also celebrate *Mundan Sanskar.*

Marriage: Saharia is an endogamous tribe but each clan in it is exogamous. Marital alliance between the mates of same *gotra* is prohibited because by virtue of their affiliation to a common totem. The Saharia practise polygamy. As among other tribal groups of state, the Saharia marriage revolves round the amount of bride price i.e. *dapa.* Generally the amount of *dapa* is settled by the parents of the prospective bride and bridegroom in consultation with village *Patels.* The most common and popular form of marriage is arranged marriage which takes place after fixing the bride-price i.e. *dapa.* They perform all the marriage rituals right from *sagai* to *vidai* at girl and boy's residence as related to them.

They also go for marriage by elopment and marriage by service in few cases.

Widow marriage is common among them. It is celebrated in a simple manner. If the widow do not marry with his *Devar,* then *dapa* is taken by her father, after that the widow can marry with her choice. Divorce is not common in this society. *Nata* is also very common in this tribal group, put the bride-price *jagha* is essential for it.

Death: The Saharias cremate their dead. For thirteen days the close relatives of the deceased stay and eat at his house. On thirteenth day, a feast is given to whole community. On the third day also, a feast is arranged for relatives only. The ashes of the deceased are put into Kapildhara or Sitabari (a pious river). When the children die, their body is burried. In special cases when the death occurs due to accidents, snake bite or some epidemic, the dead boy is burried.

COSTUMES

Male Costumes

The costumes of Sahariya man is simple. Saharia man generally wear *dhoti, Saloaka* (shirt) and a *Safa* (turban).

They wear *Chappals* rarely. Now-a-days the youngesters wear pant, shirt, and T-shirts also. The school-gooing boy use shirt, nikkar and pant. The small (infant) children generally remain naked. Even during the coldest days of winter many of them can be seen naked.

Female Costumes

Saharia women generally like colourfull costumes. There is variation in the dress of the women from place to place. In general, the dress vary with age. The women generally wear *Ghaghara, Lugdhi* and *Angi/Choli/Saluka.* Now-a-days they also wear *petticoat* and *Sari* and *blouse* also. The girls also wear skirt, blouse, petticoat and shirt. Use of *choli* is not common to young girl. Usually a women wears *ghaghara* of red or blue colour and covers half of the body upto the level of knee. The *ghaghara* requires cloth from 8-10 meter. *Choli* keeps half portion of breast exposed. *Ghaghara* and *Choli* is their traditional dress and the aged women generally wear this costume. The widow wears the same kind of dress as worn by the other warried women.

The ceremonial dress of bride and bridegroom are different. The bride wears a *ghaghara* of yellow colour and it is more decorative and costly and y ellow colour *sari* or *Odhni.* On special occasion like dances Sahariya decorate their body just like African tribal groups by various colours, leaves and feathers.

Ornaments

Sahariya man generally do not wear any jewellery. However, a few well-to-do Saharia can be seen putting on clove (long) to their cars, a *Tabij* or chain around the neck and silver buttons in their shirts.

Saharia women are very fond of ornaments. They generally wear ornaments made from gillet, aluminium or brass. Women of rich families wear silver ornaments. The most common ornaments are bore (on the forehead), *Khangari* or *hansli*, chain (around the neck), *Kanphool* or *Jhella* in ears, Silver *long* in the nose, *bara* on elbows and bangles (*mangli*) on their wrists. *Kara* and *nevari* made of aluminium is used to wear on anklet. Below it, they wear *tora.* In toes they wear *bichhia* or *chutaki* or *joria.* Unmarried girls are prohibited from the use of ornaments. They are also not allowed to use *mehandi* or to wear the brassiere like jacket, called *reja. Reja* is only wear by the married women.

Tattooing

Tattooing is one of the traditional art of adorning in tribal area. Every Sahariya woman should have tattoo mark on her body. They believe that tattoo marks enhance beauty. Every married girl must have tattoo marks of different designs. The young generation prefer tattoo on their arms only.

CHAPTER 13

Santal

Dr. Atul Chandra Bhowmick

Santal is a corruption of *Saontar* and this name was derived either from *Saont,* an obscure village in Midnapore where they ruled for two hundred years (Skrefsurd) or from a small tribe of *Saonts* in Sarguja and Keonjhar in Orissa (Dalton). The origin of Santals is traced back to a wild goose (*hasdak*) coming from the great ocean at *Ahiri Pipri* laid two eggs. From these eggs *Pilchu Haram* and *Pilchu Budhi* were produced, the parents of Santals. Their earliest abode was Ahiri Pipri santals' progenitors migrated to *Khoj-kaman*, successively to *Hara, Sasangbera, Jarpa, Kendi, Champa, Saont*, all conjectural. Santals are considered as autochthons of Santal parganas. Now they are concentrated in Hazaribagh, Bhagalpur, Singhbhum, Madhuban, Midnapore, Bankura, Purulia, Mayurbhanj, Balasore and Keonjhar.

They call themselves *Hor* (Man) *Hopen* (Son), sons of Man. They are study, simple hearted and subsist on traditional agriculture. Others work as day-labourers in colliery, industry, tea plantation and government services. Racially they belong to Proto-Austroloid stock and linguistically to Austric group.

History

The landlords exploited them miserably. Ultimately they revolted against them in June 1855 under the leadership of

Sidhu, Kanhu, Chand and Bhairab. But they were ruthlessly suppressed by the British.

Clan

Santals have twelve exogamous totemic clans (Paris). The procreation of the first seven clans were *Pilchu Haram* and *Pilchu Budhi.* The next five were added later.

Each clan is sub-divided into sub-clans (khunt/khul), whose function primarily for family deities worship. The sub-clans of *Hasdak / Hansda* (wild goose) are *Barwar,* (Eagle-slayer). *Jihu* (Babbler, a kind of bird), Kerwar, Manjhi-khil (worship at *Manjhithan*). Naeke-Naiki-Niaki-khil, Nij (oneself), Roh-Lutur (ear-pierced) and *Sada* (apply no vermilion at *puja*).

Murmu (Nilgai)—*Bital* (outcasted), Boor (Fish), *Chopear /* Coopier (Hind quarters small as bullock), *Ganr* (Fort) *Handi* (Earthen vessel). *Muro, Nij, Sada* Sanda, Sikiya (chain), Tikka (Mark on forehead and Lahar (Cut); *Kisku*—Abar, Ah, Kachua (Tortoise), *Lat* (Baked in leaf-platter), Nag (Cobra), Nij, Loh-Lutur, Sada and Somal (Deer); *Hambrom / Hemorom* (Betel-nut)—*Dantela* (pigs with large tusks for sacrifice), Gua (Areca-nut), Johur, Kumar, Laher, Naika-khil, Nij, Loh-Lutur and Uh; *Marndi / Mandi (Grass)—Buru-birit / beret (*of the hills*), (Crab), Laher, Manjhi-khil, Naiki-Khil, Nij, Roht / Roeth (Panjaun tree). Sada, Khenda Weapon* or *Sari* and *Rupa* (Silver); *Saren / Soren* (Constellation of pleiades (sorenko)—Barchi/Barchir (Sperman), Hat, Sada, Jogi (*puja* by begging, Lat, Mal, Mundu/Badar (Dense Jungle), Nij, Sankh/Sak (Couch-Shell), Sidup/Siduk Bundle or straw), Turku, Ok (Suffocation with smoke), Jihu, Bitol and Khanda (Buffalo worshipper).

Tudu—Agaria (Charcoal-burner), *Chigi / Chiki (Impale), Dantela, Lat, Manjhi-khil, Naiki-khil, Nij, Loh-Lutur, Sada* and *Sung; Baske / Baski* (Breakfast)—Nij, *Sada* sure (Cooked along with rice and Mundu; *Besra / Besera* (Hawk)—Bundra, Kahu (Crow), Kara guza (Buffalo. There are two bling brother, from their names this sub-clan begins), Nij, Sada, Sibela (Cultivated fibre yielding plant—*Groatalaria juncea* D.C.), Son, Sing and Loat (Creeper).

Pauria (Pegion), *Chero* (Lizard) and *Bedea* (Sheep)? have no sub-clans.

Earlier all clans enjoyed equal social status. But now Besra and Chero are considered inferior to other clans. Beded is deemed more lower as they could not say who was their ancestral father and is now extinct.

Nuclear and rarely Extended families are their family structure. Santals are patriarchal, and patrilineal in descent.

Life-Cycle

Birth: When a *Santal* woman becomes pregnant, the couple observe certain taboos. The husband does not kill animals, nor participate in funeral ceremonies and touch dead bodies. The wife rarely comes out of house in the evening, noon or during eclipse, cross streamlets, nor weep over death or sit on varandah with loose har.

In each child birth parents observe five day impurity. Specially prepared gruel in liberated to *Sing borga* and served to all family members. No religious ceremonies are performed in that family before performing *Janam chatiyar* rite. The wetpnurse cuts umbilical cord (*bukaw*) by an arrow-head. The cut out placenta, then buried into a pit, dug by a needle near *doorsil.* Metallic plate is rung to test the new-born's hearing ability and inform neighbours. *Janam chatiyar* is performed on fifth day and third day for boy and girl birth respectively by sprinkling turmeric, mustard oil and water taken from naeka house over new-born head. *Naeke* scatters *pituli* (Mixture of *atap chal* (Sunned rice powder with water) on feet of the male and female persons standing in rows and distributes bitter-rice to them. Then they dance and *janam chatiyar dah* for identifying whose child he is. Male child attains social right and privilege at the age of four to twelve years by performing *chacho chatiyar,* the initiation ceremony in drinking home-brewn rice-beer handia/hanriya and declared purified and attains manhood for *Jan Baha* collection of bones). Marriage is not permitted before performing *Chacho chatiyar* nor even cremated his corpse, only buries.

A *janam chatiyar dah* in their dialect

Ta kayah racha re dah bunbhukah kan

Dah bunbhukah kan mana chaole

Buhelen.

Kishuyah racha re dah bunbhukah kan

Dah bunbhukah kan mana choole

Buhelen.

(Whose courtyard is over flown with spring water. The water over-flows the rice).

The male or female child is named after the grand-father or grand-mother respectively, if they are alive. If expired, the great grand-father or great grand-mother name is assigned or when more issues. First rice giving ceremony is held in even month six or odd month seven for male or female respectively. Maternal uncle first gives rice to the child. Child is allowed to select a coin, earth lump, paddy, pen and doll, indicating its future.

Death

Santals cremate dead bodies on river banks. Children and pregnant women only buried. The dead, wrapped in a shroud, is carried by kinsmen and co-villagers and scatters parched rice and cotton seeds to avoid milignant ghosts. The corpse lays on pyre. Eldest son or in his absence, his brother puts a grass between lips and coin in his hands prior to setting it fire. Son puts a burning wood in the corpse's mouth and others kindle then the pyre. After burning charred skull piece is preserved in an urn to throw as relic into the Damodar river. A hen is nailed at corner after taken round the pyre thrice. Participants take bath and drink *handia* purchased out of deceased money. On return to the village a sheaf of leaves is hung at doorway of the dead. Participants assemble in the deceased's house to have and bathe on sixth day in *tel nahan* (oil bath) ceremony and offer earth, oil cake, oil and *sal / sarhul / sarjam* (Shorea robusta Gaertn.) twig to *Marang Budu, pitchu, Haram, Pilchu Budhi,* departed soul and his parents. The village mourns for six days and no religious rite, marriage is performed by the deceased's family. Woman who died without tattooing is considered impure and punished by Jomraja.

In the last ceremony-chandan, a he-goat is sacrified in the room where death occured. *Atap chals* are smeared with ozzes blood of a slain goat and are taken by all family members. A ceremonial feast is given signalling resumption of their normal life.

Cultural Trait

Festival (*parav*) is intimately connected with *Santal's* life and each has two aspects—(1) *Magico-religious* covering sacrifice and offerings to deities for appeasement, and (2) *Recreational* through drinking, dancing and singing. They propitiate invisible supernatural beings through exorcisms, magic and religious rites.

Their chief festival is *Sohrae / Sohrai / Goreya / Bandana,* the harvest and cattle-caressing festival, observed in last five days of *pous* (December-January), after crop harvest, Most merriest, *Jog-manjhi* entertains all, cattle are anointed with oil, daubed with vermilion and *handia* to drink. On second day each family head offers sacrifice to *Marang Budu, Orak bonga* and *Abge bonga.* All unmarried persons may indulge in promiscuous intercourse, if committed, is punishable less that at other times. Next important is *Baha,* the spring festival and *Sarhul,* both are celebrated in *Falgoon* (February-March) when sal trees blossom, indicating renewal of life.

COSTUMES

Male Costumes

Ordinarily, in daily life the Santal males wear scanty dresses. The male members at work, use only a short, course cotton *dhoti,* about four feet long, between the legs to cover the lower part of the body dangling down up to knee height. The upper part is, however, left open, usually in the hot season, but in the winter season they wear a half-shirt or a guernsey. Wearing of short *dhoti* and shirt have now come into regular use as usual attire of male Santals.

Female Costumes

The females at home wear low priced cotton bordered *sari,* usually eight cubits in length and two and a half cubits in width, half of which is knotted round the waist to cover the lower part of their bodies, while its other half is made to pass over the left shoulder covering the upper body and then it hangs in the front. They use no veils. Combed hair has a knob at the back of the head and decorate it with wild flowers and frequently with tufts of red ribbon. Young girls wear a thick cotton cloth, called *panhand,* measuring three cubits in length and one and a half cubit in width, reached up to knee height. Santal females do not use petticoat as under garment whatsoever at home. Now-a-days the young Santal women use petticoat, blouse and under-bodice with *sari.* But the old women wear only *sari.* Very minor children, generally boys move about in bare bodies. Slightly grown-up boys up to about five years wear a short loin-clothes, tied it to the red or black coloured waist thick string *danga jhinjbir/taga* hanging from the waist down to the knee joints to cover up their genital organ. Act of wearing *taga* has a belief to ward of evil eyes (*najarlaga*) to them. In the winter season, the poor Santals generally wear an additional cotton wrapper (*pichuri/chaddar*), while who afford the expenditure incurred to purchase, use a woollen *chaddar* to protect themselves from cold.

Occasional Costumes

On festive occasions and rituals, both males and females wear new clothings purchased from the local markets. But those who cannot bear the costs of expense wear washed and cleaned old clothes. Young boys wear easer pant, half-pant, occasionally trousers and shirt, while girls dressed with a under-pant and a frock, which looks like gown. At the time of marriage bridegroom wears a fine *dhoti,* coloured yellow with turmeric (*Curcuma longa Linn.*) paste, *punjabi*, an article of dress with loose sleeves vest and a conical shaped turban, soaked (gabanu) in turmeric water over his head in befitting eclat. Considering purity and for disinfection they dyed yellow the dress of the bridegroom. The marriage attire of a bride is good quality *sari,* petticoat, blouse and brassiere. Bridegroom applies vermilion from a *sal (Shorea robusta Linn.)* in bride's parted hair on forehead by right hand, usually three times or even five times, an odd number with horizontal strokes. Modern dresses, like, trousers, synthetic bush-shirt, guernsey, in the winter season woollen sweater, full-sleeve sweater, even coat rarely, shoes are creeping in the Santal society, mostly among the educated young generation. When Santals visit weekly markets they wear such modern dresses. At child birth, the new born baby wears a new shirt of light cloth, given by maternal uncle. In the pollution period due to death all members, both male and female of a family wear daily used most ordinary dresses, but washed and cleaned, not pieces of *than* as a sign of their mourning.

The dress of Santal rebels claims attention. The Santal rebels of 1855 in the Damin i-koh area was a revolt against *darogas* and *payadas* of the *thanas* for getting free from oppression of the *zamindars, mahajan* (money-lenders), *pykan* land and the *paiks* (native police of *zamindars*). On 30th June, 1855 about ten thousand Santals had assembled at Bhagnadihi under the leadership of Sidu and Kanu, who proclaimed themselves as *Subhas* (Governors). Chand and Bhairav joined their hands. The rebellion forces were dressed in short *dhoti,* tuck up the cloth tightly, hung up to knee height, tiger skin *topi* (cap) over head, *komarband* (waist-belt), made of tails of wild animals, body armour for protecting some parts of their body, smeared some parts of their body with paste of yellow or red earth, face daubed with vermilion or red colour and armed with bow and arrow, *tangi/saphari* (battle axe), *barsha* (spear), *dhal* (shield), sword and *mshal* (flambeau), some have even guns. Their head hair are black shaggy and dishevelled and eyes are ferocious. The Santal rebellion is termed by the English as *chuar/chowar* rebellion or somewhere locally known as *layek hangamma* (riot).

Santal women prefer dancing and singing almost in all ceremonial and festive occasions. *Bandana/Saharai,* a cattle caressing *parav* (festival), held after *Kali (Simasar) puja* (worship) in the month of *Kartika* (October-November), just after the winter harvest, *Sakrat* held in the last day of *Pous* (December-January), *Karam* held in *Aswin* (September-October) for increase of wealth and progeny, *Baha,* spring festival of flowers, *Chhata, Magh sim* (fowl) invoked in the month of *Magh* (January-February), held near water source and cuts a grass indicating the end of the Santal year, when dissolved the village organization, etc. festivals are held followed by dance. Both male and female participants dance together in their traditional costumes. Male members are not so well attired. They wear usually short, coarse *dhoti, payjama* (loose pantaloon) and vest, and attach plumes of peacock over head, as peacock is noted for dancing and a *panchi/gamcha* (long napkin) as a narrow head-trap with its one end hanging loosely. The female dancers, both married and unmarried are most ornately dressed in constumes, silver, brass and bell-metal ornaments. The *sari* border, mostly red passes thrice at different levels down below their hips like bands of red or blue. Red bordered *saris* are mostly used, possibly with an intention to attract the attention of viewers for its brightness. During dance, besides red bordered *sari,* now-a-days they wear printed colourful *sari* also.

Apparels thought very simple, yet these offer an exciting moment to dancers. The gathering feels happiness, peace and proudly celebrates the occasions with an idea united we prevail, united we prosper. For group dancing they rush to their own *akhra* (open dancing ground) and they all are fully geared up in the *akhra* at night-fall and continued dancing up to mid night, even to overnight-long. The steps during dancing are regular all through and the dancers entwine the hand of the just next one. The feet of the dancers take two long steps forward and next they move back with two steps of shorter nature rhythmically. They wave forward making an angle of 45° and wing to the right, while the circle appears to move in an anti-clockwise direction. They dance marrily and it is very stimulating. It is a fascinating sight and swinging up and down with a graceful lithe motion, just like wind moves the jute and paddy fields.

Ornaments

Both sexes of the Santal, specially the women-folk are very fond of ornaments. Santal women use a large variety of ornaments, which are made of silver, brass and white brass, Santal males possess different marks of cicatrization signs as customary by twelfth year on their left forearms, midway between the wrist and the elbow to divulge their tribal identity. These signs are seen on the outer side of the forearm and contain an odd number of marks as one, three, five or nine even as auspicious. The married Santal women wear *sankha* (conch-shell bangle), *loha / nowa* (iron bangle) as a marriage sign, occasionally glass bangles, *bala / todor / phora sakom (phoramud)* wrist let) around the wrist, *tard / baju* (armlet), square or rectangular big talisman as ornament, *hansuli* (necklace), *pagra* (ear-ring) for ear lobe, *khutka* with five chains of silver swinging from it for upper ear, *jhinka,* an ear-drop, *niura* (toe-ring), *nath / nolak* (nosegay) studded with coloured glass pecks, *danda jhinjhir / bicha* (waist girdle) having three silver strings fastened with a clasp, worn like a girdle round the waist with an ornamented centre shining on the back over the *sari, paina / panijor* (heavy foot anklet), one, however, wonders how an average woman carries such a heavy load of convex-shaped *paina,* a single pair weighted about 2 kg. 300 gm., worn in the legs of women, *banki / pagam / lipus* (ankle), about 900 gms. each of a pair, used mainly by newly married women, *tokli* (diadem), used at the time of marriage and *jhipjhipi,* a silver tiara-like head ornament with a crescent glimmering in a locket. Different kinds of rings are cherished by the Santal women. The most common ornament is the silver necklace. Earlier they use malla/*hara* (garland). The beads of which are made to dried ride of *bel* (woodapple-*Aegle marmelos Carrea.*) fruit bored through evenly by a needle. Santal women wear these ornaments for embellishment of self. The wrist ornament worn by women are most liked by men, perhaps because of its tinkling sounds it produce. Gold ornament is rare.

Santal women must be plump, but not fat and bear dark-brown complexion or *tel sanra* (dark-grey glaze) complexion of a *magurmach* (fish) (*Silurus Pelorius Tilions*), body straight as a stick, but not thin, with a thin waistline, hips and thighs should be fleshy and breasts, firm and hard like bel fruit for proper sex-appeal. Santals generally like women possessing an oval face with cheeks having a tendency to bulge out. And above all, women must not trot.

Tattooing

The word tattoo (Polynesian origin) is derived from to *tu*. Tattooing is very common to every Santal woman primarily with an idea of enhancing her personal beauty and to make her body graceful with such decoration. Several tattoo permanent designs are marked on skin by pricking. The simple contrivance for pricking is thorns of *bel, khejur* (Date palm-*Phoenix sylvestris Roxb.*), *Karamcha (Carissa carandas Linn.*), bainchi *(Flacourtia indica Merr.), bet (Calamus vininalis wild*). trees or porcupine quills. But in recent times metallic needles have replaced them for piercing the flesh. The professional woman, who punctures is called *khudni*.

Human milk is applied on pricked marks in the subcutaneous region by the thorn tip or needle. Then juice of the leaves of *keshurti (Eclipta alba* Hassk-*Eclipta prostrata Linn.*), a common weed is applied in tattooing and when the sore healed up leaves a permanent bluish-black tinge on skin. Often apply the juice of myrobalan (*Tarminalia chebula Roxb.*) as the dying stuff. Finally, the portion thus marked and dyed is washed with trumeric paste diluted in water as a preventive measure against infection. No separate dye is used for the purpose. Tattoo marks are found on visible parts of the body, like on both right and left wrists near the end of the forearm, forehead, neck, nose alae, cheek corner, chin and chest. They call this practice as *woolki* and wearing of *woolki* is commonly called by them as *woolkipara,* done by *baibindu* technique, generally between their ten and twelve year before marriage or before adulthood; but cases of post-marriage tattooing is done artistically, often showing the designs of flowers, variety of birds, pigeon, dot, sun, moon, diamond or any other geometric shape or even his/her name on hand. The sun symbol is presumly referred to the Santal supreme deity, *Sin Bonga* (Sun god). A Santal girl without any tattoo mark will refused generally to accept by her mother-in-law as her daughter of the house. If any woman dies without tattooing, it is a commmon belief in their society that she will be considered impure and ultimately she will be punished by *Jamraja* (God of death) and stays in hell. Besides this idea they have another belief that tattooed women have a protective power or a prophylactic against all sorts of evil spirits (*bongas*), diseases or against lustful men to seduce by means of occultism. So, Santal considers tattooing as a social and religious necessity and its omission an offence. Marks of scarification of boys and tattooing of girls, the Santals are protected against further dangers at the hands of the malignant powers in their future life and thus they keep away themselves from harm of the family.

The Santal women are very fond of flowers. They tuck invariably various coloured wild flowers in their coiffures when they go to village markets, fairs, ceremonies, religious aroma and during participation in a dance and musical soiree. They are very particular in regard to enough oiling properly their hair and its thorough combing so as to keep the hair pleated straight overhead. Bamboo or wooden comb is plugged in coiffure as hair-pin. Comb, occasionally decorated with fish figure indicates their prosperous happy married life. The married women put a vermilion mark (*tip*) on forehead between the two eye-brows at glabella and at the parting hair as signs of their marriedhood and wishing good health and long life of their husbands.

Recent changes, particularly in modern dresses of both the sexes are not wholeheartedly accepted by the elderly persons of the society as they think that a day will come soon when their traditional dresses will not prevail any more.

REFERENCES

1. Banerjee, Hemendra Nath: *Introducing Social and Cultural Anthropology,* Kitab Mahal Agencies, Calcutta, 1990.
2. Basu, Minendra Nath and Malay Nath Basu: *A Study on Material Culture,* The World Press Private Ltd.: Calcutta, 1975.
3. Bhowmick, Atul Chandra: Santal Dance, *Tribal Dances of india,* (Edited Rabin D. Tribhuwan and Preeti R. Tribhuwan), Discovery Publishing House, New Delhi, 1999.
4. Bowmick, Atul Chandra: Santal, *Ethnographic Atlas of Indian Tribes,* (Editor-Prakash Chandra Mehta), Discovery Publishing House, New Delhi, 1999.
5. Biswas, P.C.: *Santals of the Santal Parganas,* Bharatiya Adimjati Sevak Sangh, Delhi, 1956.
6. Chakrabarti, Mukul and Dipak Mukherjee: *Indian Tribes,* Saraswat Library, Calcutta, 1971.
7. Mukherjee, Charulal: *The Santals,* A. Mukherjee & Co. Pvt. Ltd., Calcutta, 1962.

8. Ray Chaudhuri, Swapan Kumar: *Ethnographic Museum—A Tribal Profile,* Special Series No. 20, Cultural Research Institute, Scheduled Castes and Tribes Welfare Department, Government of West Bengal, Calcutta, 1977.

9. Sen, Suchibrate: *The Santals of Jungal Mahals—An Agrarian history 1793-1861*, Ratna Prakashan, Calcutta, 1984.

Index